Yummy!

S

mmm....

Nom
Nom!

DELICIOUS!

yum
yum!

SWEET!

O⁰o⁰o⁰o⁰°°°o....

ow!

TASTY

Nom
Nom!

The Bank of Dreams & Nightmares
20 Rax Lane, Bridport, DT6 3JJ

www.thebankofdreamsandnightmares.org

Published March 2023 by
The Bank of Dreams & Nightmares
Copyright © 2023 The Bank of Dreams & Nightmares

Creative learning manager / Editor
Janis Lane

Volunteer story mentors
Amberley Carter
Lu Orza
Raja Jarrah
Emily England
Lizzy Rhodes
Henry Bishop
Charlie Ryrie
Lorraine Colledge
Kate Asquith
Victoria Lazarevic
Claire Shaw

Head teacher
Leif Overment

Designer
Spike Golding

Illustration
Emily Stewart

978-1-7397340-39
Printed in Exeter by Imprint books
Distributed by The Bank of Dreams & Nightmares

FOOD GLORIOUS FOOD

Recipes from
Salway Ash School,
Dorset.

INGREDIENTS

~~~

Cake

Snacks

Foreword

Food is directly linked to our memory banks. The everyday meals we make and the celebratory feasts we share represent family, heritage, generosity, and love. A bag of vinegary chips eaten on a windy beach, a green iced birthday cake in the shape of a fearsome dinosaur, a fragrantly spiced curry or a helping of the annual plump roast turkey can transport us back to our childhood as we recreate them with our own families. There is often a story behind the food we eat if only we take the time to stop and think about it.

I asked the children who took part in this fantastic BODAN project to do exactly that and consider what particular foods meant to them. They tasted ingredients representing the five basic tastes – sour, bitter, salt, sweet, and umami – and wrote about how they made them feel and the images they conjured up. The results were mind-glowingly wonderful. Each child valiantly accepted the challenge even when it was clear they hated marmite, thought chicory was disgusting or had an aversion to honey. What they wrote was inspiring, funny, informative, and thoughtful and their words encouraged enlightening and passionate discussions about the food we love.

At the end of the sessions, I asked them to help me make a 'Berrybeena' using hedgerow blackberries and wooden spoons with sleeves industriously rolled up. The cordial was poured out and we cheerfully raised our cups to each other. Now, when I make this in the future, it will remind me of those happy mornings in the school hall, surrounded by brilliant children and their amazing creativity. Thank you, pupils of Salway Ash, for giving me a wonderful memory to treasure.

Lucy Brazier
November 2022

Yummy! Scrumptious!

mmm....

DELICIOUS!

yum
yum!. SWEET!

Oooooo°°o.....

TASTY

Nom
Nom!

Glossary of Tastes

~~~

There are five basic tastes that cover all foods that we eat:

Sour
Salt
Sweet
Bitter and
Umami.

At the very start of this month-long project, food writer Lucy Brazier devised a series of taste tests for the pupils of Years 3, 4, 5, and 6, using ingredients that best showcased those five tastes. The challenge was to describe the taste, as opposed to the ingredient that represented it. The children came up with some incredible descriptions, which are summarised in our unique glossary here – all the more unique as we've put it at the start of this anthology, which is a wonderful celebration of food, and the memories we make from special moments around cooking and eating with friends and family.

Makes my eyes quiver
Teeth felt rough
Zingy
Mouth-watering
Eye-twitching
A sharp sense of loveliness
Strongly disapprove
Makes my face stretch
Tingly
Makes my teeth feel like they
crashed into a lamp post

Makes my tastebuds grumpy
Makes me shiver
Makes me thirsty
Makes my eyes wide
Tastes like the sea
Tastes stingy
Strong
Makes me think of fish and chips
Back of my mouth tingles like grit
Dissolves in my mouth

Addictive
Makes me want more
Cosy
Tastes like a flower
'Mmmmm'
Soothing
Delightful
Eyebrows go up and down
Makes me want to dance on a cloud
Plays on my tongue

I feel it in my cheeks
Scrunch your eyes up when you eat it
Interesting and glorious
Good flavour
Grassy
Itchy on my tongue
Tingly
Fresh
Buzzy on your tongue
Tastes like a stinging nettle on my tongue

Tastes like wood
Gravy with a whole bottle of bitter
Rich
Tastes like toast
Bit salty, bit vegetably, bit meaty
Goes round my throat
Aftertaste
A mixture of everything

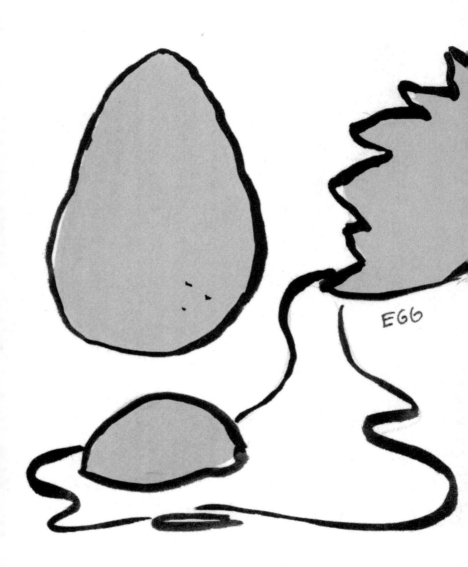
EGG

Food Stories

~~~

Appetisers

Pancakes with Syrup
by Leo

I ate half of the pancakes because I am SO greedy! My sisters only got one each, but I got four! I have two sisters. Rose is four and Edith is a baby; they like pancakes too but Edith scrunched hers up and threw it on the floor. They taste like honey but sweeter. They taste so nice and sweet and make me go hyper and I can't stop running around. Sometimes I even do the splits!

Last time I made pancakes with my daddy, he flipped the pancake over and it landed on the wall and then fell on his face! When it came down it landed in the pan and burnt. Everyone laughed except my dad!

I love pancakes and don't even feel sick after eating so many. Eating them makes me think of a funfair because the big wheel looks like a pancake. Pancake Day is when you can eat pancakes for breakfast, lunch, and dinner. They are just so squishy and juicy.

I can't wait for the next Pancake Day.

Pancake Flip
by Rosie

When I go on holiday, I go with my brother and my sister, my dad, and my mum. We camp on St Martens. I make new friends, who come to our tent and have a sleepover on the island. The people from the campsite come to my tent to play. The people come over when it's a rainy day. They come over to have pancakes; my mum makes them. I put chocolate and bananas on all my pancakes. Pancakes remind me of cake because they're like cake – yummy!

It's scary when there's a storm happening outside of my tent because all the tents are blowing away. All the children come from their tents and when there's a storm the pancakes help me calm down.

Pancakes

INGREDIENTS

100g plain flour
2 eggs
300ml/½ pint semi-skimmed milk
1 tbsp vegetable or sunflower oil, plus extra for frying

STEP 1

Put the flour in a large bowl and make a well in the centre. Crack the eggs into the well, pour in a splash of the milk and, using a balloon whisk or wooden spoon, start to stir from the centre of the bowl, drawing the flour into the eggs and milk.

Beat the mix until smooth (get any lumps out now while it's thick), then stir in the rest of the milk until it's the consistency of single cream.

Stir in the oil. The batter will keep covered in the fridge for up to a day at this point. Stir well before you use it.

STEP 2

Put a non-stick frying pan or crêpe pan (one with a 20-23cm base is ideal) over a medium heat. Pour 1cm oil into a heatproof jug and keep it to hand.

Add a drop of oil to the pan, swirl it around, tipping any excess back into the jug. Pour in a ladleful of batter, tilting the pan and swirling the batter to give a thin, even layer.

GOLDEN SYRUP

Leave the pancake alone for 30 secs, no prodding, or until it starts to colour around the edge. Don't crank up the heat if this takes longer – as you'll scorch the bottom of the pancake, and it won't flip well.

STEP 3

With a fish slice or palette knife, ease the edge of the pancake away from the pan, then loosen underneath. Check that the bottom is golden, then turn it over in one quick movement or give it a flip.

Cook for another 30 secs before turning out onto a plate. Eat straight away. Serve with lemon wedges and caster sugar, syrup or your favourite filling.

Buttery Balls
by Buddy

The last time I went to Pizza Express was last weekend. There is a big bronze horse next to Pizza Express and my sister gets angry with it, because she's six, nearly seven.

I eat dough balls and when I am finished, I lick the pot with the butter, and I have it at dinner or lunch. It is crunchy all the way through it.

I am sometimes with my brothers Zachary and Oscar, my Mum and Dad. I am 9, Oscar is 13, and Zachary is 15.

We go to Pizza Express as a special treat, birthday weekend, or after school.

Dough Balls
with Garlic Butter

INGREDIENTS

50g butter
300g strong white bread flour
7g sachet dried yeast
1 tbsp caster sugar
Oil, for the bowl and baking sheet
For the garlic butter: 100g butter and 1 garlic clove, crushed

METHOD

Warm 175ml water in a saucepan until steaming, then add the butter and set aside to cool until warm but not hot.

Mix the flour, yeast, sugar, and 1tsp salt in in a large bowl, add the cooled water to make a soft dough.

Knead for 10 mins until bouncy and smooth before returning to a clean, oiled bowl, and cover with cling film and leave to rise for 2 hrs or until doubled in size.

Oil a baking sheet.

Knock the air out of the dough and knead for a few mins.

Take small pieces of dough (walnut-sized), roll into balls, and place on a baking sheet. Cover and leave to rise for 30 mins.

Meanwhile, make the garlic butter by melting the butter in a pan and stirring in the garlic and seasoning.

Heat oven to 180°C/160°C (fan assisted).

Bake for 25-30 mins until cooked through.

Brush with some garlic butter and leave to cool for 5 mins.

Serve with remaining garlic butter, and crudités and cured meat if preferred.

Banitsa
by Eden

At Christmas we always have Banitsa. It is a Bulgarian food. It is a sort of bread with a yummy, gooey, cheese filling. My dad is Bulgarian, so we have it on special occasions, [as] it means a lot to us. We always have it with Bop soup, which is a vegetable soup. The other food we eat in Bulgaria is Shopska salad.

I have a granny and a grampa in Bulgaria, so when I eat Banitsa, it reminds me of them. I have a friend in Bulgaria that I haven't seen for a year, but we see each other on my iPad. I also have a half-sister I haven't seen before because she lives in Bulgaria.

So that is why Banitsa is special to me.

Banitsa

INGREDIENTS

30g butter, plus extra to grease
3 large eggs
125g low-fat natural yoghurt
2 tbsp sunflower oil
8 small sheets filo pastry, from a 220g pack
200g vegetarian feta, crumbled

METHOD

Preheat the oven to 200°C / 180°C (fan assisted) / gas 4. Grease a 20cm round baking dish with butter.

In a mixing bowl, lightly whisk together the eggs, yoghurt and oil.

Lay one sheet of pastry out on your work surface and drizzle over some of the egg and yoghurt mixture.

Scatter over some feta and then roll up the pastry from one of the short sides, into a cigar shape.

Place in the prepared baking dish, following the edge.

Repeat with the remaining sheets of pastry, spiralling the rolls until the dish is full.

Spoon any remaining egg and yogurt mixture into any gaps in the coil and then dot the top with butter.

Bake for 45 minutes, or until risen and golden brown.

The Creation Of The Banana Bread
by Polly

It all starts in the kitchen. Me and my family sitting at the dinner table, none of us talking. My seat is on the right facing the bananas. I look away, staring at my food. But I can't help but look at brown, almost black bananas just sitting there, no purpose. Then I can't take it anymore. I jump [up] and say the words: "we need to make banana bread!"

The next morning, me and my brother get up and start baking, weighing out the ingredients bit by bit, watching butter melt in the pan.

Next, we get out the pink bowl [and] in goes the flour bit by bit. My brother mixes it so fast it flies out of the bowl, trying to be quiet because mum and dad are in bed.

Then we take it out of the oven: you get a whiff of chocolate with glorious walnuts on the side. Then as you take a big bite, a fresh warm feeling runs through your tummy like a waterfall.

It might sound like a bad thing, but it's not filling because it's as light as a cloud.

It's so light you take a bite and all you can think about is more and more and more … and if you eat more, you still want more.

When you take a big bite, it's impossible not to smile. Me and my mum both like the end bit.

Crunch-topped banana bread

INGREDIENTS

100g butter
180g plain flour
2 tsp baking powder
½ tsp salt
150g soft light brown sugar
2 eggs
3 mashed bananas
50g walnuts
40 chocolate buttons
1 tsp vanilla extract

FOR THE TOPPINGS

2 tbsp demerara sugar
½ tsp ground cinnamon
¼ tsp ground nutmeg

METHOD

Put the melted butter in a big bowl. In a smaller bowl, mix the flour, baking powder and salt.

Stir brown sugar into the butter, then beat in the eggs one at a time. Mix in the banana, walnuts, chocolate and vanilla. Add dry ingredients and tip into tin.

For the topping, mix together the sugar with the spice and sprinkle over the top.

Bake for 1 hour then test by inserting a skewer into the centre. If the bread is done the skewer should come out clean. Leave to cool on a rack.

Oily Goodness
by Pippa W.

The last time I ate my lovely pasta was… drum roll please… was last Tuesday with my younger sister. She is six, but sometimes annoying.

Ingredients

Cayenne pepper that tastes spicy, small yellow onions that make you cry. One tablespoon of water that tastes like nothing.

Bowl

The bowl the pasta was in had colourful flowers on the inside, with the slippery goodness.

How You Eat It

You get your fork and swirl it around and then put it in your mouth.

I LOVE PASTA!

Fortnite, Forzo and Garlic Bread
by Rudy

I was playing Fortnite in my bedroom, I was eating some garlic bread. It was a garlicky flavour with a sweet taste – perhaps vinegary – I even added garlic oil to it because I made it myself. My big brother helped me put it in the oven.

I was playing Fortnite while eating the garlic bread.

My brother Merry came in and he threw a clove at me. I took some dough and slapped him on the arm. I shouted, "I AM PLAYING FORTNITE!"

I pulled out a Nerf gun and shot at him, but he dodged them all - Matrix-style!

The garlic bread tasted like Dracula on my tongue. I love the French bread. The last time I made garlic bread was yesterday. I had it with 10 KFC chicken nuggets and with some Burger King chips and a McDonald's Pepsi.

Garlic bread on a stick is my invention. We call it 'strawberry sugar legs'. It is a floppy stick of sugar and gelatine; you can bend it and eat it, though it flops around, so it is hard to munch. It is sweet and savoury.

If there was a life-sized piece of garlic bread in the room, I would dive into it.

Garlic Bread

INGREDIENTS

2 ciabatta loaves
140g butter, softened
4-6 garlic cloves, crushed
Handful of parsley, chopped
2 tbsp grated parmesan

METHOD

Slice the bread in half lengthwise.

Toast the crust side for 2 mins until crispy.

Mix the butter, parsley, and garlic in a bowl.

Spread over the cut bread halves.

Sprinkle over the parmesan cheese.

Place on a baking tray under a hot grill for 5 mins until golden.

Let it cool for 1 min before cutting into thick slices.

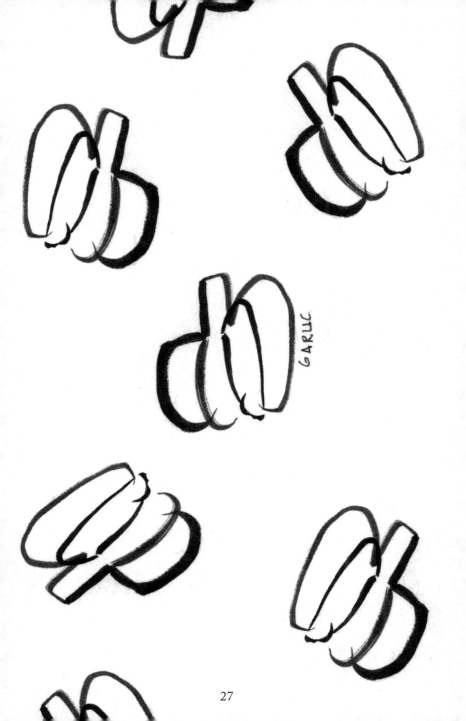

GARLIC

Odes to Food

Our young authors each composed an Ode to a favourite food. This is a lyrical poem – often quite short - that is addressed to a specific subject and written in an irregular metre.

The odes they wrote are varied, heartfelt and amusing. They are traditionally meant to be sung, but our writer's delight and love of the food being praised is clear, however you read them!

Pasta *by Pippa*

Oh, pasta,
If you were a bunny and I was a wolf,
I would eat you in one whole bite.
I love your oily slurpy goodness
and you bubble in your pan.

King-Sized Burger *by Luca*

Oh, King burger, you're so big.
I'm always so hungry for you.
It makes me feel like you are the Charizard VSTAR and I'm the
unlisted league.
You're so cheesy and greasy; you get all over my hands.
Oh, King Burger, I would marry you.

Pasta *by Eden*

Pasta, you make me smile as
you gently squish in my mouth.
My mouth waters with your cheese topping;
it makes my eyes glow in delight of the pasta sense.
I can never stop thinking of you.
I want you and your cheese topping to
come to life.

Faggots *by Zac P.*

Faggots – they make me feel warm and soft
like a hug.
You make me feel I am loved.
I feel safe when I stuff them in my tummy.

Olives *by Bella*

Oh, olive, your oily round body makes me dribble in delight.
I could eat you all day if my mum would let me!
For when I put you in my mouth, I feel like I am about to burst with happiness!
You are my favourite and I love you!

Burger *by Leo*

It has bites of gooey meat
in a golden bun.

It makes me very happy
and makes me smile.

My Ode to Pizza *by Charlie*

When I look at you,
you make me hungry.
I like the cheese and pepperoni
and I love eating you.

Pasta *by William J.*

Oh, pasta, your curly shape topped with tomato sauce on your wonderful curly shape.
When you're warm you are at the peak of your best.
When I eat you, you make me feel all warm inside.

Chicken Tikka Masala *by Edward*

Oh, chicken tikka masala, you make me feel like dancing.

Oh, chicken tikka masala, you taste amazing.

Oh, chicken tikka masala, you smell delicious.

Oh, chicken tikka masala if you could live, I would kiss you!

Food Stories

~~~

The Main Course

My Cousins Play a Trick!
by Eliot B.

When I was little, I went to my cousins' house for a sleepover. I had pasta salad with mustard, salad cream and grated carrot! They told me it was a special salad cream from a shop. So, I ate it.

The smell of the pasta was nice. It reminded me of Super Noodles.

The taste was so sweet. - I think it had maple syrup in it!

It reminded me of my grandad who died.

I think my cousins are very rude. And they lied!

Begin with Pick 'n' Mix
by Ana B.

I absolutely loved the year of 2019. I first went to Australia, and this is where I first had Zali Chicken. I loved almost all of the year apart from having to start the process of moving house. 2019 was one of the best years of my life and I loved so much of it.

Clovelly was my school and we had whole school assemblies outside. I loved walking to Clovelly because you could get lost in the high trees thinking about Zali coming to my house after school.

At Clovelly, me, and my very best friend, Zali, would laugh at the girls who sat on the steps doing their hair. We weaved nests out of sticks and made birds to sit in them.

My dog, Gwen, loves meat. She jumps up at the table, sometimes so high that she gets on the chairs to get our food. She is a Sprocker Spaniel, which is a mix of a Springer and a Cocker. She's black with a white tummy. She is fluffy and I love her most of the time.

Eating Zali Chicken now makes me feel bitter-sweet. The meal is nice, but it makes me feel sad because I miss Australia and all that was in it. The taste of it is spicy and the vegetables are like a stir-fry.

When I think of spice I think of oregano and smoked paprika pots. One of those with loads of different powder colours.

I watched this movie called Everlasting Summer. We first ate Zali Chicken in Australia and it felt like an everlasting summer. I love the idea of an everlasting summer and Australia almost gave it to me.

Me and Zali insisted that we got Pick 'n' Mix before we had Zali Chicken. We got the best variety of sweets and then played in the park. We had Zali's favourite chicken, which we then named in honour of her. Australia was the best holiday ever!

Zali Chicken

INGREDIENTS

1 tbsp oil
2 garlic cloves
1 tsp ginger
1 onion
500g chicken thighs
3 bunches of Pak choi

FOR THE RICE

180g white rice
375ml chicken stocks

FOR THE SAUCE

2 cloves garlic
4 tbsp hoisin sauce
4 tbsp soy sauce

METHOD

Mix all of the sauce ingredients in a large bowl, add chicken to marinate for a few hours or overnight.

Cut Pak choi stems into thick slices.

Heat oil in a large pot over medium high heat. Remove chicken from marinade shaking off excess. Reserve remaining marinade.

Cook both sides until golden – about 90 seconds on each side.
DON'T LET THEM BURN!

Remove the chicken onto a plate.

Add a touch of oil if the pot is dry. Add onion, garlic and ginger.
Cook for 2 mins until tinged with gold.

Add rice and stir to coat the grains of rice in oil. Add stock, reserved
marinade and Pak choi stems.

Place the chicken across the top, bring to simmer. Lower heat
to medium.

Cook for 20-30 mins or until liquid is absorbed.

Remove from heat, scatter Pak choi leaves across surface and put
the lid back on.

Rest for 10 minutes, then serve.

Tacos
by Nathaniel B.

When we first went to a taqueria I was a bit nervous, but my dad told me how to put in the fillings, and when the meat fell out, he told me it was supposed to be like that! Tacos at home are always the best ones because you can make your own ones with any ingredients that you want and leave out the fillings you don't like!

The tortilla is salty and crunchy and made of the same stuff as crisps (which I eat every week and tacos only once a month).

My favourite ingredient is beef and soured cream because I like the taste of them together.

I like them because I like the things inside.

Taco Terror (*a tiny tale by Nat)*

One time, there was a giant nuclear bomb factory…on fire! …AND THE WORLD EXPLODED! But the explosion combined with a taco that the man was eating. The world was now a taco world!

DUN DUN DUUUUN!

Tacos

INGREDIENTS

450g lean ground beef
1 cup chunky salsa
10 taco shells
½ iceberg lettuce, shredded
1 medium tomato, chopped
1 cup grated cheddar cheese

METHOD

Cook the beef in a pan until brown, then drain the liquid.

Stir the salsa into the pan.

Heat to boiling and reduce to medium-low.

Cook for 5 mins then turn into a serving bowl.

Heat taco shells as per instructions, put them out alongside the beef.

Create a toppings bar of lettuce, cheese, and tomato. Additional toppings such as avocado, peppers, sliced radishes, and more salsa are delicious too.

Build your tacos!

Tomato soup family
by Sivatia

My name is Sivatia, I do the stirring. My sister licks the spoon. My dad chops the stuff up. What are we making? Tomato soup! Onions, tomatoes, tomato juice and water.

I pick the tomatoes in the front garden. We don't have a greenhouse; they grow in pots on a shelf. It smells really weird when you pick them. I can't decide if I like the smell or not. I put them in my Easter basket like I'm collecting Easter eggs!

When my dad chops the tomatoes, I put my hand on his and my sister puts her hand on mine.

The tomato soup is not smooth, it's lumpy. I don't like the skin or the seeds but it's okay because you don't taste the seeds.

Me and my sister eat it in our bedroom. Mum and Dad eat it at the dinner table.

When I was four, we all made tomato soup and I fed it to our dog! I felt really naughty. The dog liked it. It ate it all and was not sick.

The soup is hot, and America is hot, so it reminds me about America. I go every year.

Tomato soup

4 servings

INGREDIENTS

4 cups diced or pureed tomatoes, canned or fresh
2 fresh scallions, finely cut, stem and bulb
¼ teaspoon dried thyme
½ teaspoon dried basil
½ teaspoon parsley, finely chopped
½ teaspoon salt
⅛ teaspoon pepper
½ cup of milk
½ cup of water (optional)

METHOD

Simmer the tomatoes, scallions, thyme, basil, parsley, salt and pepper together for 30 mins. Add ½ cup of water.

Heat but do not boil the milk in a large saucepan.

Slowly pour the tomato mixture through a strainer into the milk, stirring all the time.

This is delicious hot or ice cold.

Chicken Katsu Curry
by Abigail

I love rice and chicken. I tried it at Wagamama's in London. I got chicken Katsu curry without the side salad because I only like the chicken and rice.

The rice is fluffy. We make it at home from the cookbook, but the sauce comes out too spicy, more than in the restaurant.

It makes me feel as happy as if it was my birthday, even though we don't have it then.

Chicken Katsu Curry

FOR THE CHICKEN

400g chicken mini fillets or 2 chicken breasts, cut into strips
1 tbsp plain flour
1 free-range egg, lightly beaten
100g/3½oz dried breadcrumbs
3 tbsp sunflower oil
Jasmine rice, to serve

FOR THE SAUCE

1 onion, chopped
1 carrot, chopped
1 tbsp sunflower oil
2 garlic cloves, crushed
2 tsp grated fresh ginger
1 tbsp medium curry powder
1 tbsp plain flour
500ml/18fl oz chicken stock
1–2 tbsp soy sauce
Salt and freshly ground black pepper

METHOD

To make the sauce, put the onion, carrot and oil into a saucepan and cook over a low–medium heat for 4–5 minutes. Add the garlic, ginger and curry powder and cook for a minute, stirring often. Add the flour, mix well and cook for a further 30 seconds. Gradually add the stock, stirring constantly. Bring slowly to the boil, reduce

to a simmer and cook gently for 10 minutes until smooth and thickened. Season to taste with soy sauce, salt and pepper.

To prepare the chicken, tip the flour onto a plate, the beaten egg onto another and the breadcrumbs onto a baking tray.

Coat the chicken fillets in flour, shake off the excess, then dip into the beaten egg to coat and shake off any excess. Put the chicken into the breadcrumbs and turn so that each piece is evenly coated.

Heat the oil in a large frying pan over a medium heat. Add the chicken pieces and cook for about 3 minutes on each side, or until golden.

Serve the crisp chicken with steamed rice and the hot curry sauce poured over.

The Gurt Lush Poor Man's Pie!
by Bella

Bristol is where most of my family live and is where my mum came from. Most of it is roads and buildings; there are lots of shops and most of them are crowded. And there is one very special person to me and that is my Nana June!

My Nana June is very kind and loving and is a very good cook. She spends half the day in the kitchen and my favourite is her Gurt Lush Poor Man's Pie! If you are wondering what 'gurt lush' means, then I will tell you; it means big and lovely. They also say it's 'mint', which means cool!

She created this delicious food one day with the stuff she had left in the cupboard.

The crispy pastry makes me feel loved and warm inside, and I love the way the meaty meat makes me want more. Sometimes if you are lucky, you get a little slice of cheese and bread, but you have to be fast to get a slice, because my Nana June has 10 children, 24 grandchildren, and 29 great grandchildren!

It is special to me because it is her own recipe, and she would always tell us a story about her childhood whilst I eat it. I find it interesting how different it was back then. She once told me that when she was 7, she didn't know what a banana was and she ate it with the skin on and now she eats one for breakfast every day.

And that is why I love Poor Man's Pie.

The End.

Great Nana June's Poor Man's Pie

INGREDIENTS FOR THE FILLING

500g minced beef
1kg potatoes for mashing
2 white onions
1 pot of gravy granules

FOR THE PASTRY

450g self-raising flour
225g of margarine
1-3 tbsp of water at room temperature

METHOD

The filling

Peel potatoes, place in a saucepan of unsalted water, bring to the boil and then let simmer until tender.

Place the minced beef in a separate saucepan with 2 diced onions. Fill with water then bring to the boil and let simmer for 25/30 minutes.

When the potatoes are done, drain and mash until light and fluffy.

Once the mince is ready, add the gravy granules gradually and stir constantly.

Once the potatoes are mashed and the meat is done, slowly add the mince to the potatoes and mix together.

POTATO

ONION

The pastry

Add the margarine into a bowl.

Then add about half of the self-raising flour and mix with your hands until you get a bread crumb texture.

Next, add the rest of the flour into the bowl and carry on mixing with your hands.

Once you have a bread crumb texture, add the room temperature water gradually until you get a smooth texture.

Sprinkle the surface with flour.

Separate your pastry in half and roll out one half to fit your dish.

Grease the bottom of your dish and place the pastry into it.

Final part

Now, fill the dish with the filling.

Then, roll out your other half of pastry and pop it on top.

Then, put it in the oven at 150°C.

Nana June always says that if you have any pastry left over, make jam tarts!!

Shepherd's Pie
by Charlie J.

I like eating with my mum because I don't spend that much time with her. Sometimes my little sister joins us as well – she is two soon. It feels nice to spend time together as a family.

I like homemade shepherd's pie more than one bought in a shop. It tastes better because my mum makes it really good. She puts cheese on it and puts it in the oven, and it gets all crispy.

Shepherd's pie has meat and gravy in the bottom, and potatoes on top. The meat is my favourite part. It's very good. The potato part is a bit boring.

Shepherd's pie makes me feel hungry again even if I've already had dinner. I always want seconds. I feel like I could eat it forever.

[I like to eat shepherd's pie in my room]. My room is at the back of the house. From the window I can see the garden with my trampoline and the pool. I can see my cat. I like to be alone in my room and watch stuff on TV when I eat.

Veggie Shepherd's Pie

INGREDIENTS

700g potato, 225g red onion, 1 carrot, 1½ cartons of chickpeas
90g cheddar cheese
225ml basil
1 sachet dried oregano
2 sachets sun-dried tomato paste
1 sachet red wine stock paste
40g grated hard Italian style cheese

METHOD

Put a large saucepan of water with ½ tsp of salt on to boil, chop potato into 2cm chunks and boil for 15-20 mins.

Halve, peel, and gently slice the red onion, mushrooms and trim and grate the carrot.

Heat a drizzle of oil over a high heat in a large frying pan and add the onion and mushroom. Season with salt and pepper and cook for for 7-8 mins until soft and starting to brown. Drain and rinse the chickpeas. Put half the chickpeas in a bowl and mash with a fork until broken. Grate the cheddar.

Pour the tomatoes, water, oregano, and tomato paste. Add the red wine stock paste and stir to combine. Stir in the grated carrot and chickpeas until the mixture is simmering and cook with the lid off until the sauce is thick and tomatoey, 10-12 mins.

When the potato is ready, drain in a colander and return to the pan off the heat. Add a knob of butter and hard Italian style cheese and mash until smooth. Season with salt and pepper. Preheat your grill to its highest setting.

Spoon the mix into an ovenproof dish and top with the mash. Smooth with a spoon and sprinkle on the cheese. Pop in the grill until the cheese is golden and bubbling for 2-3 mins and serve.

Glorious Steak Pie
by Edward

When we go shopping, I ask mum, "Can we have my steak pie?"

If she says, "Yes, we can," we put it on the list. When we get home, I get the recipe book and mum grabs the ingredients. We put all the ingredients in a pot, and we cook it. Next, we make the suet pastry. Once we have made the [pastry] lid, we put the filling in, pop the lid on, and finally cook it in the oven. When it is finished in the oven, I open the door and the delicious smell of steak pie goes up my nose and it alerts me that it's ready.

I make it every winter because it makes me feel warm before bed. I eat it for dinner with my mum, dad, and my sister, Heidi, in our kitchen-dining room. I eat it with broccoli, carrots, and sometimes gravy.

It all started with a Year 2 homework, when we had to find an old recipe. I mostly have it as a treat; it is so sensational that it makes my mouth water.

Steak Pie

INGREDIENTS FOR FILLING

1-2 tbsp beef dripping or cooking oil
450g chuck steak, cut into 2.5cm cubes
225g ox or lamb kidneys, cut into 2.5cm dice
2 carrots, roughly diced
2 onions, roughly diced
2 celery sticks, roughly diced
175g button mushrooms, quartered
300ml stout (optional)
600ml beef or veal jus, or alternative
1 bay leaf
1 quantity suet pastry
Salt and pepper

INGREDIENTS FOR SUET PASTRY

300g self-raising flour
150g shredded suet
200ml water
Salt

METHOD

Heat a frying pan with the dripping or oil; fry the beef and kidneys in stages, browning well.

In a separate large saucepan, fry the vegetables in a touch of oil.

Cook for a few minutes, then add the stout if using.

Bring to the boil and reduce by two-thirds.

Add the jus and bring to a simmer. Add the bay leaf.

Now add the beef and the kidneys, cover, and cook for 1-1½ hours.

Adjust the seasoning and leave to cool.

For the suet pastry, sieve the flour and salt together in a mixing bowl.

Add the suet, breaking it into the flour.

Stir in the water to make a fairly firm dough.

Roll out on a lightly floured surface.

Line a pudding basin with 1-2cm hanging over the edge.

Reserve some pastry for a lid.

Drain the stewed beef and veg, reserving the cooking liquor.

Remove the bay leaf and spoon the mixture into the pastry-lined basin.

Add just enough sauce to barely cover.

Put the pastry lid on and fold in the excess edges.

Top with folded, buttered foil, wrapping it around as you would with parchment paper, twisting it to hold.

Stand in a steamer filled with hot water and cook for approx 1½ hrs.

If you don't have a steamer stand the basin in a large saucepan of boiling water covered with a tight-fitting lid or foil.

While the pudding steams, simmer the remaining cooking liquor to make a gravy.

Turn the pudding out and pour over the gravy to serve.

American Burgers
by Lois

I ate them in America in a hotel called Mandalay Bay, in Las Vegas. It was plated in gold. I always ate them with my 15-year-old brother, my 18-year-old brother, my mum, and my dad. I also have a dog, but sadly he couldn't come on an 11-hour flight.

I love when they have bacon in, and the tomato and lettuce make it so fresh. They are the size of my head, and they never have a kids menu – it's crazy!

You can have bacon, cheese, lettuce, tomato, onion, pickles, and even sausage.

You can also customise how much the burger is cooked as well as what's in it; you can even have nothing in it.

I don't remember a time it didn't come with chips.

The 11-hour flight was not fun – it was so long, and NO Wi-Fi and the food smelled horrible and wasn't nice.

The best holiday ever!

Botham Burger

Serves 4

INGREDIENTS

1kg minced beef
2 medium red onions, finely chopped
2 eggs
1-2 handfuls of fresh breadcrumbs
1 tbsp crushed coriander seeds
1 pinch crushed cumin seeds
1 heaped tsp Dijon mustard
Salt and ground black pepper

METHOD

Preheat oven to 230ºC.

Mix and scrunch ingredients together.

Use breadcrumbs to bind and lighten mixture.

Divide the mixture into 4 and mould each burger into small cricket ball sized shapes.

Place in oven and roast for 25 mins so the middle is slightly pink, and the outside is more crispy.

Serve with a bun, salad, salsa, and ketchup.

Sushi
by Lowri

I feel so lovely when I make it.

I don't know why I am jumping up and down whenever I see it.

On my dad's birthday, I made a big mess. On my birthday I had to pick up sushi.

I once made a mess with the sushi.

It is so amazing I could fall off my chair!

I feel so happy inside because it is so good.

I like making sushi because it's my favourite and you can get messy hands.

Sushi

FOR THE RICE

300g sushi rice
100ml rice wine vinegar
2 tbsp golden caster sugar

FOR THE JAPANESE MAYONNAISE

3 tbsp mayonnaise
1 tbsp rice wine vinegar
1 tsp soy sauce

FOR THE SUSHI

25g nori (seaweed) sheets
Fillings: cucumber, salmon, white crabmeat, tinned tuna,
red pepper, avocado, spring onion

TO SERVE

Wasabi
Pickled ginger
Soy sauce

METHOD

To make sushi rolls, lay a nori sheet on a bamboo rolling mat.

Dip hands in vinegared water and pat rice down on the nori sheet to
1cm thickness, leaving a gap at furthest edge of the sheet.

Spread a thin layer of the Japanese mayonnaise over the middle of
the rice.

Top the line of mayo with the filling(s) of your choice.

Lift the edge of the mat to roll it up, applying pressure to keep it tight.

Brush the clear edge of the mat with a little water and continue rolling to seal.

Remove the mat and wrap the roll tightly in cling film.

Cut the sushi into slices, then remove the cling film and serve.

To make pressed sushi, line a loaf tin with cling film and layer smoked salmon on the lining.

Press approx 3cms of rice over the salmon and press down.

Tip out the sushi like a sandcastle, cut into fingers, and remove the cling film.

To make sushi balls, take a small square of cling film and place a topping on it.

Use damp hands to roll a walnut-sized rice ball and place on the topping.

Bring the corners of the cling film together and tighten the ball by twisting.

Serve all sushi with wasabi, pickled ginger, and soy sauce.

Chicken Nuggets and Chips
by Blaize

I have them at dinner-time with my family. They are a treat! They are crunchy on the outside and soft on the inside. I like salt on my chips.

Chicken Nuggets

INGREDIENTS

75g plain flour
1 medium egg, beaten
100ml skimmed milk
½ tsp onion salt
500g skinless chicken breast
Salt and ground white pepper
Vegetable oil for deep frying

METHOD

Sift 50g flour into a bowl and make a well in the centre

Add the egg and gradually blend in the milk to form a smooth batter

Season with onion salt

Cut the chicken into 3-4cm pieces and put in a bowl

Sift the remaining flour onto the chicken and add seasoning

Mix well till all the chicken is dusted with flour

Heat the oil in a deep fat fryer or large saucepan to 180°C (365°F)

Pour the batter over the floured chicken and mix gently so all pieces are covered

Using tongs, lower 6 or 7 pieces of chicken into the hot oil for about 7 mins, turning occasionally, until golden all over and cooked through.

Chips *by Cecily*

When you chew a chip, its crunchy goodness melts.
When you put salt and vinegar on a chip
and put it in your mouth it explodes.
And what if you put chips with fish?
It adds more deliciousness.

Ode to Tacos *by Nat*

Oh Tacos, when I eat you
I feel like I am in heaven.
Oh Tacos, you go so well with black beans.
Oh Tacos, when I eat you, I feel like you are multiple.

Noodles *by Mia*

Oh, noodles, I will miss you when I eat you,
Oh, noodles, if you could talk, I would take you on a date.
Oh, noodles, I would take you everywhere I go, even to school.
When you are going in the microwave,
when I am looking at you.
I want to go swimming with you.
Oh, noodles, I would go shopping with you.

Roast Beef *by Willow S.*

Roast, I love roast
I wish I could have it
every single night
BUT WITH NO CARROTS!

Roast Dinner *by Louie*

Oh, roast dinner, when I buy you, I want to eat you frozen.
Oh, roast dinner, you make me happy.
Oh, roast dinner, I want to eat you every day.
Oh, roast dinner, I love you –
I could stuff you in my mouth all at once.
Oh, roast dinner, I love you and I want to eat you
At snack, lunch, and dinner time.

Chicken Schnitzel *by Ana*

Chicken Schnitzel when I first saw you, I was unsure.
Since my sister and dad had made you and promised galore.
Yet down on the beach
(where you were first to be eaten),
I dipped you in the special dip and lifted you to my mouth.
The first bite is mere inquisitiveness.
But with growing wonder, the sesame seed breadcrumbs fell away
in my mouth,
the soft tender chicken that alights in my throat.
Oh, schnitzel, with you as chicken, surely,
I must be fox, as your goodness is only to admire.
I just can't resist.
You are the best; you just beat the rest.
Chicken Schnitzel, you couldn't be better.
If only my dad had not blended the seeds,
but now to forget I must eat as I please.

Pizza *by Joseph*

You make me want to have all your flavours.
You make me so happy when you are freshly cooked.
Wherever you are you bring happiness to me,
and I don't need anything on you.

Lettuce *by Flori*

O' lettuce, O' my darling lettuce,
Every time I open the fridge door,
I see your gleaming green eyes;
I smile and am delighted.
Instead of going to the cinema with sweets
I will always want to take you.
I want to take you on a date in the fridge
and maybe marry you some day.
Every time I eat you, you take my breath away.

Lasagne *by Buddy*

Oh, lasagne, I love the cheesy crispy bits and
the layers of meat and crisp.
You smell cheesy and
crispy and you make me feel happy.
You make my tummy hot.

Pizza *by Jasmine*

Pizza, I love you.
When I eat you, you have a very sweet and savoury taste.
Your small, thin crusts are very tasty and very crunchy.
I would give you a 10/10.
You're so sweet; we're really good friends.
I wish I could eat you.
You have very good taste.

Fajitas *by Spike*

Oh, fajita, you burst my tastebuds with joy.
I hope you'll be my valentine.
You make me want to cry.

Cottage Pie *by Archie*

Cottage pie is good because of its mashed potato and lentils.
It is very good with meat or lentils.
When I eat it, it makes me feel happy because of the nice taste.

Burrito *by Thomas*

I love a burrito.
Its white crusty edge wraps around the glorious, juicy meat
while beans, tomatoes, cheese, and pepper add to the sensation.
When I dig my teeth into it,
it makes me fall into another world.
As it goes down into my stomach,
I feel like the happiest person alive.

Tuna *by Elliot*

Oh, tuna, you are the best food in the world, you're lovely.
If you could talk, I would marry you.
You are very nice.

Steak *by Rudy*

Steak! Your beautiful beefiness
looks good in the medium rare.
Seasoned with salty pepperiness,
your mixture of tastes is excellent.

Cheeseburger *by Archie L.*

Oh, cheeseburger, you're better than any other burger;
I will eat you day in day out.
When I bite into you, I feel like I'm in heaven.
You are the best when you are from Rise;
You are amazing.

Roast Dinner *by Felicity*

Oh roast dinner, you make me feel so hungry
Oh roast dinner, me and you are like a fox and bunny
Oh roast dinner, when I stuff you down in my tummy
Oh roast dinner, if you were alive, I would kiss you in my belly.

Ode to Chips *by Abigail H.*

Oh chips, I love you.
You make me feel hungry.
You go so well with burgers.
I love you with salt,
Ketchup – when you are hot –
I love you!

Yo Sushi *by Ted*

Yo Sushi,
your different fillings with your rice and pepper.
Wrapped in seaweed with your soy sauce fried in fish.
While being different shapes, after you come out of the ocean,
you know you're going to be in my stomach one day.

Burger *by Guy*

Oh, burger, your lovely seedy bun
and your terrific, crispy lettuce, and your exquisite, oily meat.
Once I start eating you, I just can't stop;
all of your lovely red ketchup drips onto the plate.
Your lovely burger juice fills me up with joy.

Sausage *by Albert*

O' sausage, you make me happy
I love your taste.
It's yummy.

Food Stories

Dessert

When Skeletons Come for Dinner
by Felicity R.

Halloween reminds me of sitting with a skeleton, me as a vampire and two regular humans sitting around my table eating pumpkin pie with cream and maple syrup. As we gut the delicious home-grown pumpkin, I feel murderous but also feel sorry for all the animals that could have eaten this instead of us.

Dressing up has a very old loft smell. When we get them out of the box there are a hundred laughs and giggles while trying to squeeze into old costumes made by grandma and given for Christmas when I was princess obsessed. When we have face paint on, we are usually eating pumpkin pie, so you have to be careful when you're eating it. The smell of the paint reminds me of the day that Dad was at home making the pumpkin pie whilst mum picked me up from school. Then we went into Bridport for a surprise. It was new face paint from Instant Redress.

Warm spices are the powder of Autumn. They smell, taste, and look like an avenue of trees with their leaves cascading onto our heads. I just can't resist throwing a huge handful at my sister as she reaches down to collect an acorn.

The loud sound of the blender spooks the kittens and they scamper angrily away from the sound that has just ruined their chances of licking the butter. As the soft pumpkin becomes a puree, Alma runs around the house telling Dad to turn off the blender so she can continue her dance party with her teddies.

Cinnamon reminds me of my kitchen in pumpkin pie baking mode with the cats and dogs around our feet trying to pickpocket some butter (that's still out, making our kitchen even messier than it already is).

Maple syrup mixed with fresh cream is a wonderful side dip for a warm pumpkin pie after a cold day at school.

Apple Pie
by Braxton

Apple pie makes me happy because it is happy. It tastes like crumble and apple at the same time.

The apple tastes sweet like pie.

It was a Wednesday because my Nan made it. It was all crumbly; it was like the plate was eating it.

Nan collects lots of apples. She gets them from Grandad, who sneaks around and collects them from the neighbour's garden!

It's nice and crumbly and the apple juice squirts into your mouth. I have my apple pie by itself because it's nice enough on its own. I eat it warm because it gives me a warm feeling; when you're cold it warms you up straightaway. It's soft in some places and hard in others.

It reminds me of my family when Nan makes it.

Apple Pie

INGREDIENTS FOR THE FILLING

150g caster sugar
1 tsp ground cinnamon
2 tbsp cornflour
600g Bramley apples, peeled, cored, and sliced

INGREDIENTS FOR THE PASTRY

400g plain flour, plus extra for rolling
2 tbsp caster sugar
1 lemon, zest only
280g cold butter, cut into cubes
1 egg beaten with 2 tbsp cold water, plus 1 beaten egg to glaze

METHOD

Place the flour, sugar and lemon zest into a bowl and rub in the butter cubes with fingertips.

When it resembles breadcrumbs, add the beaten egg, and stir to form a dough.

Set aside one-third of the pastry for the lid.

Roll out remaining dough on a lightly floured surface to thickness of a pound coin and approx 2 inches larger than the pie dish.

Lift the pastry over the rolling pin and gently lower the pastry into the dish, press in firmly.

Chill for a few minutes.

Preheat the oven to 200°C/180° fan and place a baking tray in to preheat it.

Mix the sugar, cinnamon, and cornflour in a large bowl.

Stir in the apples.

Place the apple filling in the pie dish.

Brush the rim of the dish with beaten egg.

Roll out the reserved ball of pastry.

Cover the pie and press the edges together.

Trim any excess pastry and crimp the edges.

Make a few holes in the centre of the pie with a knife, and glaze with beaten egg.

Make leaf shapes from pastry offcuts to decorate the pie.

Sprinkle with sugar and bake in centre of oven for 45-55 mins.

APPLE

Finishing Up a Finnish Dessert
by Alice

Each time we have it, it's a sensational feel whilst it slowly disintegrates in your mouth. Every time we have it there's a special tradition we always do: we always have to try not to lick our lips. I'm always the first to give in but that means I get to be the judge.

The wondrous smell filters the air just like a strong expensive perfume. It leads you into a trance you can't get out of. Someone always manages to get it on their nose, and everyone laughs when they do. They try to touch their nose with their tongue to get the cream off, but in the end, they end up using their finger.

Cream is the best filling. A fluffy cloud dances on your tongue, disintegrating slowly into a warm, sugary melt.

Laskiaispulla

(15 servings)

INGREDIENTS

2 cups of milk
50g yeast, or 3 tablespoons of dried yeast
¾ cups of sugar
150g butter
1 tablespoon ground cardamon
5½ cups of flour

METHOD

Microwave butter to soften it to room temperature.

Mix yeast with lukewarm milk.

Dissolve the yeast into the milk. Add sugar, butter, cardamom, salt and 1-2 cups flour. Beat into a batter.

Add rest of flour and knead. Add butter when dough gains elasticity.

Knead for 7-15 mins until firm.

Let the dough rest. Cover bowl with a cloth and let dough rest in a warm place for 20 mins.

Make into 15-16 round buns by kneading them against surface of palm.

Let buns rise to double the size.

Brush with beaten egg.

Bake at 400°F [200°C] for 14 mins.

Let it cool down.

Slice in half and fill with ½ tbsp of jam or marzipan and add whipped cream.

September Pudding
by Flori

September is the month me and my mum go blackberry picking (any other month and the blackberries won't be ripe). We always go picking in my village, by the pub with a huge river.

We pick them together and it has been a special thing we have done since I was four years old. We know not to pick the red and green ones and only pick the big juicy ones. We have a competition to see who can get the most in their tub. (I always win). We bring litter-pickers to get to the ones we can't reach.

When we get home, I peel the apples and mum washes the blackberries. Then mum cooks the apples whilst I pour the food into the bowl. After it is all cooked, we pour the breadcrumbs onto the apple and blackberries.

We eat it together in the dining room. We have it with honey, squirty cream, and ice cream. The crumble is crunchy, but the apples and blackberries are soft.

Crumble
by Leah H.

I go to Pymore to pick some blackberries with my mum, dad, and Riley. My fingers go purple with the juice. We don't eat any because they are all for the crumble! We buy apples on the way home.

Dad and Riley peel and chop. Mum and I mix butter, flour, and sugar to make the crumble. It is sticky and greasy; I don't lick my fingers – UGH!

We play while it cooks and I am very, very excited. Mummy makes custard; it is yummy. It smells like apple and blackberry and also smells lemony. While it's cooking it makes my mouth water. Dad gets the plates, and we all get a big bit - except Riley.

Amazing Apple Crumble
by Amelie

Every Autumn I love to pick apples from our two apple trees. One is big and one is small, the apples are green and red. When I take them off the tree, I always feel the pull of the apples on the tree branches.

Every Christmassy, cold day in the holidays or not, I love to make apple crumble for my family. When I go up to Scotland to meet them, I instantly know it will suit the holiday, winter snow perfectly.

When I meet my family in Pitlochry or Aberdeen (Scotland), I love to spend time with my Auntie having sleepovers. And with my cousin, playing football, sledding, having snowball fights and going to the park. I usually go every year to Pitlochry and West Hill (Aberdeen).

When I am preparing the crumble, the smell in the air of sourness hits my nose. But weirdly when it's cooking it begins to smell sweeter and when it's done, I can't wait to eat it. When I'm thinking of it, I am yearning to eat it.

It smells so warm and yummy. I love it with hot custard and when I eat it, it makes me even warmer. I love to eat it in a blanket on the sofa while drinking hot chocolate. I love it so much!

When I eat it, I taste the lovely, sweet taste in my mouth. When the warm steam rises, the steam smells so good wafting up my nose making me want to eat so much more.

When I eat it, it crunches in my mouth, the sweetness overwhelms me every time.

Warm Hedgerow Bounty
by Oscar

My sister is four and a half, and I'm nine and a half.

I have to walk two miles to get to the field to pick the apple and blackberries. I usually have to chase the cows away, as they always want my blackberries.

When I have apple and blackberry crumble, I have it alone in my bedroom. The crumble is very mouth-watering, so good it makes me feel like I'm in a sewage pipe. I like it with funky banana ice cream, that I first tasted in Bideford.

Once when I ate it, my dad was singing a really stupid song. My sister was laughing so much she flapped her arms and knocked over the candle, which fell on the crumble. It caught fire and the fire engine turned up and put it out. We had to eat burnt crumble. I stuffed it in my face.

I like the crusty crumble, it's just so crumbly.

Thanks for listening to my crumble story.

THE END.

Apple and Blackberry Crumble

INGREDIENTS

120g plain flour
60g butter
60g sugar
300g apples
30g demerara sugar
115g blackberries

METHOD

Heat the oven to 190°C.

Add the flour and sugar to a large bowl.

Add the butter and rub into the flour using your fingertips to make breadcrumbs.

Sprinkle mixture over a baking sheet and bake for 15 mins.

Peel core and cut apples.

Put the butter and demerara sugar in a medium saucepan and melt together, cook for 3 mins.

Stir apples and blackberries in the mixture and cook for 4 mins.

Serve a spoonful of warm fruit in a bowl with crumble mix and ice cream.

BLACK
BERRIES

Too Long to Dry
by Ava

I love Christmas because of the tree. But I (also) love the chocolates, the hardness at the inside and the drizzle on top. Me and my auntie make them at Christmas at my home for the whole family of seven people.

We make them in the kitchen, and it takes an hour to dry. They take so long to dry but I cannot wait to eat them. They are hard in two ways - hard to make, and hard on the inside.

My favourite is the one with the red dots. In the middle is hard chocolate. My dogs sit next to me when I eat them.

Hand-dipped chocolates

INGREDIENTS

90g ready-to-roll fondant icing
Rose & violet flavourings
60g white marzipan
6 Brazil nuts & 6 whole almonds
30g dark chocolate
30g white chocolate
30g milk chocolate
6 Maraschino cherries & 6 Crème de Menthe cherries
Crystallised rose and violet petals

METHOD

Cut fondant into 2 pieces.

Flavour 1 piece rose and colour pale pink and the other piece violet and colour mauve.

Roll out the fondant to ½ inch thickness.

Cut into shapes using cocktail cutters.

Place on wax paper-lined baking sheet.

Shape marzipan into various shapes by rolling between hands.

Arrange on baking tray and leave to dry for several hours or overnight.

Toast the nuts.

Melt each chocolate in different bowls over hand-hot water.

Using a fork, dip one of the dried centres into the chocolate, tapping to remove excess.

Press nuts into centres first, or use nuts as a centre on their own.

Place on baking parchment-lined baking sheets.

Leave chocolates plain, or decorate with a fork or crystallised rose and violet petals.

You can also pipe some chocolate threads over the top.

Chocolate Pizza
by Conrad

I first made and ate chocolate pizza with my professional baker of a sister, and it tasted like ground sugar in my mouth. She cooked it in the Kitchen of Death.

When I went into London Zoo, I first saw a bird-eating tarantula. The mere colour of it reminded me of chocolate. When I first watched the Teenage Mutant Ninja Turtles movie, Raphael's suit reminded me of chocolate pizza. Raphael is a ninja turtle, mutated, and REALLY strong. The Indoraptor's colour reminded me of a chocolate pizza. The Indoraptor is a genetically modified dinosaur in Jurassic World. I've no idea why the Indominus Rex also reminds me of chocolate pizza, it just does. The Indominus is a part gecko, part T-Rex and raptor hybrid dinosaur, also from Jurassic World.

Chocolate Pizza

(Makes one pizza)

INGREDIENTS

200g Melted chocolate
4 Digestive biscuits
1 Flat bread
1 Banana (sliced)
Plus 5g of the secret ingredient not to be divulged
(sprinkled on top)

METHOD

Mix warm water and yeast in a small bowl to blend. Let it stand still until yeast dissolves, about 5 mins.

Mix flour and salt in a food processor to blend. Blend in the oil. Add the yeast mixture while the machine runs and blend until the dough forms.

Turn the dough out onto a lightly floured surface and knead until smooth, about 1 min. Transfer the dough to a large bowl and turn it to coat with olive oil. Cover the bowl with plastic wrap and set aside until the dough doubles in volume for about 1hr. Punch and form into a ball.

Position the oven rack on the bottom of the oven and preheat the oven to 230°C.

Line a heavy large baking sheet with parchment paper, roll the dough to a 9-inch diameter round. Transfer dough to prepared baking sheet. Make indents over the dough with your fingers. Brush the dough with butter and bake until the crust is crisp and pale golden brown, about 20 mins.

Immediately spread the chocolate hazelnut spread over the pizza and sprinkle the chocolate chips over. Bake until the chocolate begins to melt and sprinkle the hazelnuts over the pizza. Cut into wedges to serve.

Banoffee Pie Time
by Florence P.

My mum makes Banoffee Pie while I play on my tablet. I can smell it – lovely fumes wafting upstairs. We cook and eat the Banoffee Pie in the kitchen. I constantly come down and ask if it is ready or not.

I love the Banoffee Pie. I eat it at Christmas. It makes me so happy when my mum makes it. We have Christmas at Nana's and at Dad's, our house, and in Scotland. In the morning, Mum and Dad go downstairs and check to see if there are any presents. Then we open the presents. It's my favourite part of Christmas Day. In the evening, after we have Christmas dinner, we have the Banoffee Pie. It's good, but not as good as opening presents!

I'm so happy when I eat it, I forget where I am. It's so yummy I feel like I'm on clouds. It tastes of toffee and bananas. It's really sweet, and we have it with whipped cream.

Quick Banoffee Pie

INGREDIENTS

250g digestive biscuits, crushed
100g butter, melted
397g can Carnation Caramel
4 small bananas
300ml carton whipping cream, whipped
Grated chocolate to decorate

METHOD

Mix the crushed biscuits with the melted butter thoroughly.

Press the mixture into a loose-bottomed 20cm round cake tin.

Chill for 30 mins.

Use a spoon to spread the caramel onto the biscuit base.

Slice the bananas and cover the caramel with them.

Put the cream on top and decorate with grated chocolate.

Chill until ready to serve.

Doughnut *by Alice*

Sweet, sweet doughnut,
I would eat you forever if I could.
You're the perfect sugar doughnut but
with icing and sparkles, you're even better.
If you were a mouse and I were a cat,
you would be gone in one second.

Ice cream *by Felicity B.*

To ice cream,
I love you
I could eat you every day
You're lovely and delicious
I love you in all my heart
When I eat you,
it makes me feel loved.

Berries *by Kit*

Berries, o' berries,
Your sweet taste,
Like I'm a wolf and
you're a rabbit…
Berries, o' berries, you're yummy.

Brownie *by Martha*

Oh, brownie, how I wish
to eat you; the chocolatey mess
inside you brings a warm
comforting feeling.
Oh, how you taste like heaven; it's an inexplicable feeling.
I always want more.

Trebor *by Sivatia*

O' Trebor, you are minty and white.
You are like a moon but smaller
and you make me feel happy.
It is crunchy, then it goes soft.

Chocolate *by Ava*

Oh, chocolate,
I like when you are mint.
I want to run but when I ate dark,
I died.

My Ode to Noodles *by Bayleigh*

Oh, noodles, you're so long, so delicious.
Just like a snake and I'm the stoat – mmmm
So good, I would marry you if I could…
Oh, you're so good; I would eat you so much.

Chips *by Conrad*

Your long, delicious fingers make my mouth water so much,
I think I might drown.
Oh chippy, my mate, I hereby eat you.
Here's a little song in your honour…
Super chip, super chip, you're the best and I'm going to eat
yooooooooouuuuuuu!
A cannibal's heart would MEEEELTTTT!
Here's to your being – and a statue of you,
my Lord Chippy.

Pancakes *by Amelie*

Oh, pancakes,
how I love to watch you bubbling in the pan.
When you flip over your brown side is revealed.
The sweet honey dripping off the stacks,
the soft, bumpy textures in my mouth with lemon and sugar
or Nutella or lovely butter cubes.
The circularness of your perfectly round shape.
You are like a cylinder of yumminess.
When I eat you, warmness enters me,
The brown and yellow; when I see you
I want to scream YAY!
You taste so good
and your smell wafts up my nose...
Oh, how I couldn't live without you!

Macarons *by Polly*

Macarons,
I love your light bubbly outside and your white,
creamy middle that melts in my mouth.
Your outside is like biting into a cloud, and the fact
that you come in so many different colours and flavours...
If I could, I would make my house out of you and have
macarons every course in a day.

Blackberries *by Lowri*

To Blackberries,
you taste amazing.
I could eat all the blackberries
in the world.
If I was sick,
I wouldn't care at all.

Ode to Chocolate Twirl *by Blaize*

Oh Twirl,
you make
me dribble.

Yummy! Scrumptious

mmm....

Nom Nom!

DELICIOUS!

yum yum!. SWEET!

Oooooo°°.....

Now! Nom Nom! TASTY

Food Stories

Cake

The Perfect Sponge
by Ted

The first time I made microwave syrup sponge was when I was 7, but that was three years ago. You can make this glorious dish in less than 10 minutes. The texture is spongey, squishy on my tongue, and above all it is very hot.

All the syrup sauce smells sweet and sugary. We buy the ingredients from Lidl or Morrison's and then make it at home. I make this on the weekends when all my family is there, and we always have it after dinner at the table.

I make this in the evening with my mum and stepdad and we serve it with cream and ice cream. All of my family loves this dish: that's me, my two older sisters, my younger sister, my mum, and my stepdad.

Microwave Syrup Sponge

INGREDIENTS

125g butter
125g caster sugar
2 eggs
150g plain flour
1 tsp baking powder
2 small lemons, zest and juice
1-2 tbsp milk
2 tbsp golden syrup
Custard

METHOD

Grease 1-2 litre bowl.

Sieve flour and baking powder, tip sugar, eggs, butter, and baking powder into food processor and mix into paste.

Add lemon juice and zest, mix, and add enough milk to reach a dropping consistency.

Spoon the mixture into the bowl and cover with cling-film and microwave on full power for 4 mins.

Leave to stand for 2-3 mins then turn it out and serve with custard/golden syrup.

Put the cream on top and decorate with grated chocolate.

Chill until ready to serve.

Rainbow Cake is Yummy!
by Mia D.

For my birthday I had a big, big, big rainbow cake. It was very yummy. I ate rainbow cake with Billie; she is my best friend. We will go to the same big school – Beaminster Big School.

Me and Billie went down a big, big, big, big, big water slide.

Me and Billie went swimming down the Leisure Centre.

Me and Billie went on the climbing wall together.

Me and Billie went to Fellows Cove. I went down the death slide.

Me and Billie went to the beach together; we had a swim.

Me and Billie went camping together in our field.

When I was at Diggerland, I went on the big ride.

Me and Billie went to lots of parks.

It made me happy.

Rainbow Cake
by Harrison

I had rainbow cake for my birthday. My Mummy, my Daddy, and my sister were there. She is 13 and I am 7. When I baked the cake, it smelled like chocolate. It smelled really sweet.

I blew the candles out. Sometimes I blow out the candles for my mum, my dad, my sister, Clive, my granny, Jess, and Nanny, on their birthdays too!

It is called a Rainbow cake because there is a rainbow inside. This is done by using loads of food colouring, which comes from a tiny bottle.

The cake was yummy. My favourite part is the icing. It was a bit sweet, but I felt very happy.

Rainbow Cake
by Felicity G.

It's my seventh birthday and I am so excited. Mum said I could choose whatever I wanted for my birthday cake. Rainbows are such a lovely sight in the sky, I decided I wanted one for my cake.

At home, Mum found some eggs, sugar, butter, and flour for the cake. And five bowls for the five colourings: red, orange, yellow, green, and blue.

Mum cooked them in five different cake tins. The red one smelled like strawberries, the orange like oranges, the yellow like banana, the green smelled like grass, and the blue like blueberries! The strawberry was my favourite; my mouth was watering.

When the cakes were done, my mum hid them away from me. I went to bed wondering what my cake would look like the next day. While I was asleep, Grandma snuck in!

Mum and Grandma decorated the cake. There was yellow for a beautiful fairy's golden hair and blue for a silky dress. She had sparkly gold wings and a trail of glittery fairy dust. She was magical.

In the morning, my naughty sister Eloise said, "Felicity, I know where your cake is! Come and see it."

I ran downstairs with her. My cake was on the kitchen side. Mum and Grandma said, "Happy Birthday Felicity! We hope you have lots of fairy wishes."

For my next birthday I would like a lying-down-unicorn, rainbow cake – that was what my birthday wish was!

It made me feel full of magic.

Rainbow Cake

(Makes 6 coloured sponges, two at a time)

INGREDIENTS

125g butter, softened, plus a little extra for the tin
225g plain flour
150g golden caster sugar
2 large eggs
1 tsp baking powder
Pinch of salt
1 tsp vanilla extract
Edible food colourings (red, blue, orange, yellow, green, purple, optional pink) to finish

FOR THE ICING

1 tsp vanilla extract
750g soft cheese or mascarpone
350g icing sugar

METHOD

Put the butter into a bowl with the caster sugar, flour, salt, eggs, baking powder and vanilla extract.

Beat, using a hand-held electric mixer, until light and creamy.

Divide the mixture equally between two bowls.

Add red food colour to the first bowl and orange to the second and yellow to the third.

EGG

Add only ¼ tsp of colour at a time until you reach the desired shade. Mix well.

Pour each bowl of sponge mix into a prepared tin and spread to level.

Bake both in the oven for 12–15 mins, or until firm to the touch. Turn onto a wire rack to cool.

Using the remaining cake ingredients, repeat the process twice more, to make four more sponges. Colour these yellow, green, blue and purple/pink. We prefer pink.

To make the icing, put the butter and cream cheese into a bowl and beat until smooth.

Add half the icing sugar and mix well. Then, add the remaining icing sugar and beat until smooth.

Place the purple sponge on a cake board or plate and spread with a little icing. Place the blue sponge on top. Continue layering this way, following the colours of the rainbow. Spread the remaining icing around the sides of the cake and chill until firm.

My Chocolate Cake
by Diggory

My mum makes it most of the time and on my birthday. It smells lovely when it comes out of the oven. It smells so warm: a sweet smell. It is yummy and sweet in my mouth when I chew it. The sponge is nice and squishy and moist. My favourite is the gooey bit in the middle and the top. When I chew it, the wet gooey sponge and the bit in the middle and top all stick to my mouth. It makes me smile when I bite into the sweet, thick, squishy sponge. I eat my chocolate cake with my mum, dad, and sister.

I Finally Got the Brownie
by Martha

The chocolate cake recipe was my Grandad's but now it's mine. In my family, for birthdays, whenever we are going to make a cake, we make a chocolate cake or a Victoria sponge. I like both and can make both. It's yummy in my tummy.

My grandad is a baker. He makes warm yummy bread also – white, brown, or even with seeds in.

My Dad used to like brownies so much we couldn't eat them.

"But I've made you a chocolate cake," said grandad.

"Oh, OK you can have a brownie," said Dad.

So now we can. It makes me happy and smile when we eat them; it makes my mouth water, so chocolatey and delicious, and when it's warm it is (even) more yummy.

Chocolate Cake

INGREDIENTS

225g plain flour
350g caster sugar
85g cocoa powder
1½ tsp baking powder
2 free-range eggs
250ml milk
125ml vegetable oil
2 tsp vanilla extract
250ml boiling water

FOR THE CHOCOLATE ICING

200g plain chocolate
200ml double cream

METHOD

Preheat the oven to 180°C. Grease and line two 20cm sandwich tins.

Place all the cake ingredients in a large bowl except the boiling water and beat the mixture until smooth.

Add the water to the mixture a bit at a time until smooth.

Divide the mixture between sandwich tins and bake for 25-35 mins.

Remove the cakes from the oven and allow to cool.

For the icing heat the chocolate in a pan with the cream on a low heat until it melts and remove from the heat. Whisk until glossy and smooth. Set aside for 1-2 hours.

Run a round bladed knife around the inside of the cake tins to loosen the cakes. Remove from the tins.

Spread a little icing over the top of one cake and top with the other cake.

CHOCOLATE

My Apple Cake Disasters
by Bayleigh

When I was making apple cake with my mum, I chucked the pan on the floor in anger, and liked it anyway.

I remember I stole the apples from my neighbour's garden, and he chased me to Pitchers, but I ran to the Secret Way. It was worth it because [the apple cake] tastes so good.

It tastes of apple and really nice plain cake, with loads of sugar.

Once I slipped over and chucked apple cake all over Oakleigh. I took it off his face and ate it. Oakleigh is my brother. He's 11.

The first time I had apple cake, my granddad gave it to me before he died, and I have loved it ever since. My brother hates making it, but he loves eating it.

Apple and Blackberry Cake
by Kit

My granny cooks the apple and blackberry cake because she likes cooking with me. We both love cooking (though the pizza I cook, I burn it!). I help her make the mashed blackberries and the apple sauce. I squish the apples and blend the blackberries.

The juiciest apples are from the garden, and we have the biggest, juiciest blackberries. I love the cake; it's sweet, with a good texture.

Apple and Blackberry Cake

INGREDIENTS

125g butter, softened, plus extra for the tin
125g caster sugar
3 large eggs, beaten
50g ground almonds
100g self-raising flour
2 Discovery, Russet, or Worcester apples, peeled, cored, and cut into 12 segments
100g blackberries

FOR THE TOPPING

1 large pinch cinnamon
2 tbsp demerara sugar
25g butter, cut into flakes
25g peeled and toasted hazelnuts, roughly chopped
Icing sugar, for dusting

METHOD

Heat oven to 160°C/140° fan.

Butter and line a 22cm loose-bottomed cake tin.

Beat the butter and sugar together until light and fluffy.

Gradually pour in two-thirds of the eggs and beat, adding a little flour if it curdles.

Fold in the remaining egg, then the ground almonds, then the flour. Combine gently.

Add two-thirds of the apples to the mixture, and all the blackberries.

Turn the mixture into the tin and smooth gently.

Scatter remaining apples on the top.

Sprinkle over cinnamon, demerara sugar, and butter.

Bake for 50-55 mins until a skewer comes out clean.

Remove and scatter with the toasted hazelnuts.

When cool, dust lightly with icing sugar and bake in centre of oven for 45-55 mins.

No Cake
by Guy

One of my favourite cakes I have made was a really nice, gooey brownie. But the fruit loaf was my favourite because it wasn't very unhealthy, but it was just as sweet. It was one of my favourite cakes I have made.

At home I made it with my mum; well, she soaked the fruit in the tea, and I did the rest. It tasted even better when it was warm because the fruit was very squishy. It made me feel happy and it warmed me up from the inside out.

I brought it to Cub Camp; it was really fun. I didn't get to sleep until 3.00am. Cub Camp was four whole days long, but it was really fun because there was a lake in the next field along. We got to bring our own cake that we made because we had a slice of cake every morning. It was really annoying because I didn't get to eat any of it as I left a day early and they had it on the last day!

Fruit Loaf

INGREDIENTS

170g sultanas
170g raisins
Zest of 1 orange
360ml tea
2 eggs
250g self-raising flour
200g brown sugar
Butter

METHOD

Mix the sultanas, raisins, and orange zest in a large bowl.

Pour over the tea and leave overnight.

Heat the oven to 180°C.

Add the eggs, flour, and sugar to the mixed fruit, making sure everything is combined.

Spoon the mixture into a loaf tin and cook for 1½ hrs.

Leave to cool in the tin for 15 mins before turning out.

Good Cake
by Archie L.

My home is good. It is homey when something is cooking.

We have lots of grey doors and windows. I like to watch TV when the cake is baking so the time flies.

Sticky strawberry jam. I like eating it at the end.

I always eat the cake after my dinner.

My mum is really nice. She feeds me and keeps me alive.

I like to spend time with my family and eat cake.

The actual thing is cake, so I like it. The cake is so yum, I could eat it all day.

Marble Cake
by Lettie

On my 8th birthday I had three cakes; two were a Pokémon marble cake and one was a M&S strawberry cake. My next one might be a Harry Potter marble cake.

My mum made it for my birthday last year and now I want it for every birthday because it is delicious and looks amazing. I even like thinking about it. I like looking at the patterns and you never know what patterns you will see.

I like making all of it, but my favourite bits are decorating and making patterns, and my sister (who is four), always licks the bowl.

Marble Cake

INGREDIENTS

225g butter
225g caster sugar
4 eggs
225g self-raising flour
3 tbsp milk
1 tsp vanilla extract
2 tbsp cocoa powder

METHOD

Heat oven to 180°C and grease cake tin and line it with greaseproof paper.

Put the butter, sugar, eggs, flour, milk, and vanilla extract into a mixer and beat until smooth.

Divide the mixture between two bowls and stir 2 tbsp cocoa powder into the mixture in one of the bowls. Take 2 spoons and use them to dollop the mixes into the tin alternately.

Take a skewer and swirl around the tin to create a marble effect.

Bake for 45-55 mins.

Lemon Drizzle
by Henry

Granny helps to run a tea and cake house.

My favourite bit of lemon drizzle cake is the jam on it. I think it's the sweetest bit. The sugar is tingly and feels like sand in my mouth. You might think that it is sharp like a knife, but it isn't.

Once at the beach my mum warned me that a big wave was coming: I looked, and it splashed on the cake!

I also like chocolate cake.

The First Time I made Lemon Drizzle!
by Jacob

For my birthday I made it in my kitchen with mum and dad. I asked to make it because it tastes so yummy.

I could hardly wait for it to cook; I was bouncing on my feet like a hopping bunny. My mum kept asking me to stop.

Every time I lay it in my mouth, I can smell the sweetness of the lemon icing. Last time I ate it, I remember the icing crunching in my mouth.

My heart pumps because I love it so much.

Lemon Drizzle Cake

INGREDIENTS

225g unsalted butter, softened
225g caster sugar
4 eggs
225g self-raising flour
1 lemon, zested

METHOD

Heat oven to 180°C/160°Fan.

Beat together butter and caster sugar until pale and creamy.

Add eggs one at a time, slowly mixing.

Sift in the flour, then add the lemon zest and mix to combine.

Line a loaf tin with greaseproof paper, then spoon in the mixture and level with a spoon.

Bake for 45-50 mins until a thin skewer comes out clean.

While the cake is cooling in the tin, mix lemon juice and caster sugar to make the drizzle.

Prick the warm cake all over with a skewer or fork, then pour over the drizzle.

Leave in the tin until completely cool, then serve.

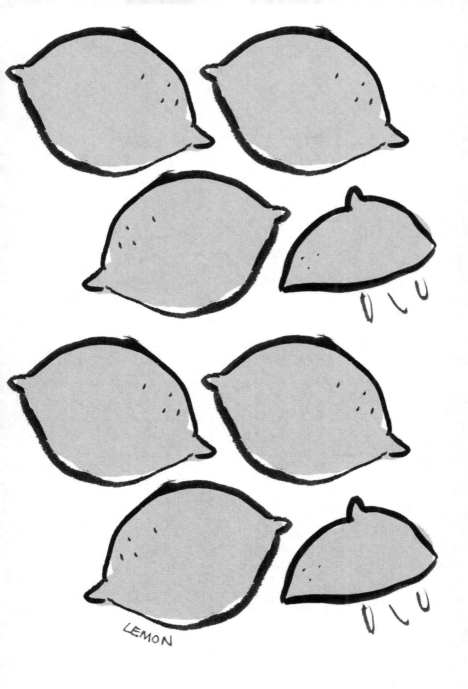

LEMON

Size of Slice
by Alice

My dad always likes milk chocolate cake on his birthday. We have it at least once a year. We had it last April. It's from the Be-Ro book that my dad used when he was a child. My dad loves chocolate and that's why this is his favourite. It reminds me of Easter because his birthday is near Easter.

The wonderful smell of gooey melted chocolate makes your mouth water while it's cooking. We always eat it in the warm light kitchen filled with house plants. We sit at our long wooden table with chewed seats (because my dog Milo chewed them - he is a Sprocker spaniel). Everyone always fights over the biggest piece. It makes like the richest, most melt-in-your-mouth chocolate.

It makes me happy because it makes my dad happy.

Milk Chocolate Cake

INGREDIENTS

200g self-raising flour
225g caster sugar
½ tsp salt
25g sieved cocoa powder
100g margarine
2 medium eggs
5 tbsp evaporated milk
5 tbsp water
Few drops vanilla extract

METHOD

Heat oven to 180°C.

Grease 2 x 20cm tins (not loose-bottomed).

Mix flour, sugar, salt, and cocoa.

Rub in the margarine.

Beat the eggs with the evaporated milk.

Add the egg mixture to the dry ingredients with a few drops of vanilla extract, and stir to combine.

Pour the mixture into the prepared tins and bake for 30-35 mins.

When cool, sandwich the cakes together and top with milk chocolate icing, chocolate fudge icing, or chocolate buttercream.

Pickles cake
by William S.

My mum wanted a cake, so I baked one. It was not sunny, so I baked it on my own. It is so spongey. You have one layer of sponge, cream and jam and the next bit of sponge. It is Mum's favourite cake.

It was the first cake I baked. Now I have baked some more. I have baked muffins, carrot cake, and lemon drizzle. And I once gave my guinea pig, Pickles, a strawberry from a cake!

I think the most fun cake to bake is lemon drizzle. I like it because it's easy. It makes me smile because it's so delicious. It makes me go 'yum!'

Victoria Sponge

INGREDIENTS

175g butter, softened
3 medium eggs, beaten
1 tsp vanilla extract
175g self-raising flour
1 tsp baking powder
4 tbsp raspberry or strawberry jam
Icing sugar for dusting

FOR THE BUTTERCREAM

50g softened butter
125g icing sugar
½ tsp vanilla extract
2 tsp milk

METHOD

Preheat oven to 180°C.

Grease and line 2 x 20cm cake tins.

Place the butter, eggs, sugar, and vanilla extract in a large bowl and sift over the flour and baking powder.

Beat all ingredients together until thick and divide the mixture between the two tins, levelling the tops with the back of a spoon.

Bake in the centre of the oven for 25-30 mins, or until risen and firm.

Leave the cakes to cool for a few minutes before turning out onto a cooling rack.

To make the buttercream, place the butter, icing sugar, vanilla extract, and milk in a mixing bowl and beat with a wooden spoon until smooth and creamy.

Spread the flat side of one sponge with jam, and the other with buttercream. Sandwich the two together, and dust with icing sugar.

Cake *by Jacob*

Gimme your brains.
Gimme your body.
Gimme your home.

Brownie *by Alice S.*

Oh, brownie, how I wish to eat you;
the way you fill me up with joy is
inexplicable.

Your chocolatey goodness
brings a warm and
comforting feeling.

You make me want to melt
inside your gooey mixture.
You just make me want more.

Cake *by Lynton*

Oh chocolatey iced sponge cake.
You make me smile.
I'd eat you whenever I could.

Cake *by Henry*

My favourite cake is lemon drizzle cake.
I love the jam.
O' Jesus, thank you for inventing lemon drizzle cake.

Ice Cream *by William S.*

Oh, ice cream, you make me feel so cold on a hot day.
All your flavours make me feel so happy.
My favourite one is raspberry pavlova with a bit of meringue.

Lotus Biscuit *by Daisy*

Oh, lotus biscuit,
I love your crunch,
You are small and bumpy edged,
When I see you, I think 'Yay!'
If I take a bite all I can think of is coffee.

Crunchy Crunchy Crisps *by Violet*

O' crisps,
every time I open you,
I get a whiff of cheese and onion in my face.
Your crunchy inside fills me with joy.
O' crisps,
your blue packet is so eye-catching
when you are in that big box of other crisps.

Cucumber *by Letti*

Cucumber, you make me smile.
When I bite into you it
takes me into my mind.
Your lovely, juicy, watery taste
makes me think of my favourite places.

BREAD

Food Stories

Snacks

Cookie Dough
by Joseph B.

My memory is at Christmas with everyone round the table.

At my house we all make something each and put it on the table to share. I make cookie dough.

Cookie Dough

INGREDIENTS

A handful of Chocolate Chips
200g sugar
100g butter
200g flour
A pinch of salt

METHOD

(Due to the risk of e-coli in flour, it is a good idea, before starting, to heat treat the flour by microwaving on full power for 1 minute 15 seconds, stirring every 20 seconds).

Cream the flour, butter, sugars and salt in a mixing bowl.

Using an electric hand mixer whip mixture until pale and fluffy (about 3 minutes).

Finish with the chocolate: Add the chocolate chips then fold in with a rubber spatula to incorporate.

The Delicious Muffins
by Louie

What do you need to make a muffin? Butter, eggs, oil, milk, flour, sugar AND chocolate drops. I get all the ingredients with Mummy. I am so excited!

Everyone in my family is involved. Mummy melts the butter, Daddy gets the whisk out and my sisters mix it. I crack the eggs! My sisters take it in turns to mix the batter. It is gooey and sticky; it looks delicious already. We add the chocolate drops, and we eat some too!

Daddy gets a spoon and puts the batter in the cupcake holders. He makes a real mess. Mummy says, "Tidy it up, Ryan!" So, he must do the clearing up. Oh no!

Now in the oven to cook for 20 minutes. I watch them while daddy clears all the batter up. We lick the bowl; we have a spoon each so there's no fighting!

My tummy rumbles when they are getting bigger, and it makes my mouth water.

Then they are ready, hot, and spotty with chocolate drops....Mmmm.

Muffins

INGREDIENTS

2 medium eggs
125g vegetable oil
250ml semi-skimmed milk
250g caster sugar
400g self-raising flour
1 tsp salt
100g chocolate chips or dried fruit

METHOD

Heat oven to 200°C/180°Fan and line two muffin trays with muffin cases.

In a large bowl, beat the eggs lightly.

Add the vegetable oil and milk, and beat till combined.

Add the sugar and mix to a smooth batter.

Sift in the flour and salt and fold in. Take care not to overmix.

Stir in the chocolate chips or fruit.

Fill the muffin cases two-thirds full and bake for 20-25 mins.

Leave to cool for a few mins before transferring to a wire rack.

Golden Syrup Flapjacks
by Felicity B. (with Willow P.)

"Mum, please can we make some flapjacks?"

"Sure, but you need to get all the ingredients out with me."

We walk into the kitchen. Me and my mum make it nice with lots of syrup, yummy, delicious golden syrup, and jumbo porridge oats. When I smell, it smells like syrup.

The shiny bits are where the golden syrup is, which makes me feel happy. I look at it in a daisy cake tin. I like it with strawberries and raspberries. When I eat it, it tastes like fresh honey from the bees. I make it so delicious!

Golden Syrup Flapjacks
by Willow P. (with Felicity B.)

A few weeks ago, my family were making them for somebody else and I couldn't have one. I said, "Our neighbour won't need that many - her cats will eat them," but my mum still said no. I ran around the house, cranky, and then ran into the kitchen and ate one.

Whenever I smell or see the flapjacks, I rush downstairs and beg for some, while bouncing up and down on the sofa.

I love golden flapjacks because they remind me of the fresh, delicious honey from the bees and I make them at my house.

I love them because I make them with my mum.

Flapjacks
by William J.

We got the recipe from Colfox [School] because my brother was doing Food Tech. Sometimes me and my brother go to see our favourite football team in London and watch them play together. After that we walk around London.

Oats are one of things that you don't eat on their own, but you only put in stuff - they go into flapjacks.

I want to taste the mixture before it goes into the oven to cook but my brother doesn't let me. My favourite part is the chocolate – melted chocolate is the best part of the flapjack because of the sweetness.

I always get excited because of the wisp of smell going up to my bedroom. I run all the way downstairs. It makes me happy because of the sweetness of the flapjack; it makes me feel warm because I eat it just after it comes out of the oven, and the golden syrup is gooier and stickier instead of hard.

Flapjacks
by Willow S.

Granny brings flapjacks to swimming. It makes me smile because she makes them.

They smell sweet when they come out of the oven. They are sticky because there is syrup in them. They taste like chicken skin. Flapjacks are yummy because they are sweet.

Flapjacks

INGREDIENTS

225g porridge oats
110g hard margarine/butter
85g sugar
2-3 tbsp golden syrup

METHOD

Heat oven to 180°C. Lightly grease your tin.

Measure the syrup in a saucepan using a tablespoon.

Add butter and sugar into a pan and warm on a low heat on the hob until dissolved, stirring gently all the time. DO NOT let it boil! Turn off the heat when the butter is melted.

Remove the pan from the hob and stir in the porridge oats.

Place in tin and flatten slightly. Press down around the edges.

Cook for 15 mins until golden brown.

Remove from the oven and let cool on a cooling rack.

Cut into portions.

Leave to cool completely before removing from the tin.

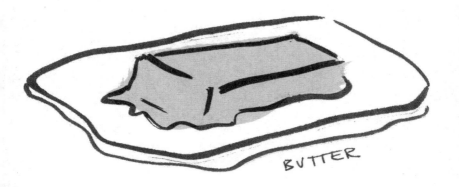

BVTTER

The Men Arrived
by Archie C.

I don't remember it myself, but my mum and sister tell me that I made gingerbread men at Christmas with my sister. I used to call gingerbread men 'Gerald' because I was bored with waiting for them to get cooked.

When I cook them, they are crunchy because I cook them for a long time. I like them with icing. I also put dry icing on and cook it for half an hour. It makes me dribble because the icing is lemony and the chocolate is also tasty.

I leave them out for Santa and in the morning they are gone.

Christmas Gingerbread Men

INGREDIENTS

350g plain flour, plus extra for rolling
1 tsp bicarbonate of soda
2 tsp ground ginger
1 tsp ground cinnamon
125g butter
175g light soft brown sugar
1 free-range egg
4 tbsp golden syrup
Writing icing & cake decorations

METHOD

Sift together the flour, bicarbonate of soda, ginger, and cinnamon.

Add the butter and blend until it looks like breadcrumbs.

Stir in the sugar.

Lightly beat the egg and golden syrup together, add to the main mix and pulse/combine till it clumps together.

Tip the dough out, knead briefly until smooth, wrap in clingfilm and refrigerate for 15 mins.

Preheat the oven to 180°C and line two baking trays with greaseproof paper.

Roll out the dough to ¼ inch thickness on a lightly floured surface.

Cut the dough into desired shape by hand or using a biscuit cutter.

Place the cut dough onto a lined baking tray and bake in the oven for approx. 10 minutes.

Carefully remove the biscuits from the oven and place on a wire rack until completely cooled.

Decorate with icing as desired

Gone in Seconds!
by Thomas

It all started with my mum making the cookies, then my sister helped out, then I was interested and every now and again my brother helps. It's really fun.

When I come home after school, I am always tired and hungry. You must know how I feel after a long day. When I open the biscuit tin and see the golden, crispy cookies it makes me smile.

When they come out from the oven the warm air blows into my face. They are always nice and warm. When they are warm, they taste delicious and amazing.

The cookies taste even tastier when they are soft and gooey in the middle. The chocolate melts on my tongue and the cookie crumbles into my stomach.

This tasty treat always reminds me of Lockdown. All the lovely times at home with my dog, Luna.

My dog, Luna likes to sit on my lap and have a nap. When she wakes up, she always wants me to give her a tummy rub.

One time though, Luna jumped up and snatched a cookie out of my grasp. She was very ill and was very quiet. She eventually got better and never tried to snatch a cookie again.

I used to have a Golden Retriever called Molly. She always tried to protect me when I was younger. I remember the times eating cookies next to her.

Cookies remind me of the summer. I eat the cookies, then I do my outside activities. It brightens up my day.

Cookies

INGREDIENTS

150g salted butter, softened
80g light brown muscovado sugar
80g granulated sugar
2 tsp vanilla extract
1 large egg
225g plain flour
½ tsp bicarbonate soda
¼ tsp salt
200g dark and milk chocolate chips or chunks

METHOD

Heat the oven to 190C/fan170C/gas 5 and line two baking trays with non-stick baking paper.

Put 150g softened salted butter, 80g light brown muscovado sugar. and 80g granulated sugar into a bowl and beat until creamy.

Beat in 2 tsp vanilla extract and 1 large egg.

Sift 225g plain flour, ½ tsp bicarbonate soda and ¼ tsp salt into the bowl and mix it in with a wooden spoon.

Add 200g dark and milk chocolate chips or chunks and stir well.

Use a teaspoon to make small scoops of the mixture, spacing them well apart on the baking trays.

This mixture should make about 30 cookies.

Bake for 8-10 mins until they are light brown on the edges and still slightly soft in the centre if you press them.

Leave on the tray for a couple of mins to set and then lift onto a cooling rack.

Marmalade
by Luca

Grandma lives down Pineapple Lane. There are lots of flowers at Grandma's house. I haven't seen her in ages. I always make delicious marmalade with joyful Grandma. She makes it fun.

We make marmalade in the summer. We need a lot of oranges to make marmalade and once we start doing it there is a bowlful of pips on the side.

Paddington always keeps a marmalade sandwich under his hat.

Whenever I hear the popping of the toaster, I rush to get more.

I am always hungry for marmalade. Sometimes, I eat it straight out of the jar.

"Don't eat it straight from the jar!" says Mum.

Marmalade

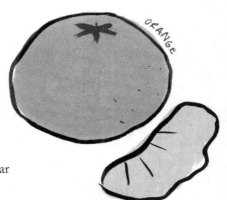

INGREDIENTS

1.3kg Seville oranges
2 lemons, juice only
2.6kg preserving or granulated sugar

METHOD

Put the whole oranges and lemon juice in a large preserving pan and cover with 2 litres/4 pints of water. Bring to the boil, cover and simmer very gently for around 2 hours, or until the peel can be easily pierced with a fork.

Warm half the sugar in a very low oven. Pour off the cooking water from the oranges into a jug and tip the oranges into a bowl. Return cooking liquid to the pan. Allow oranges to cool until they are easy to handle, then cut in half. Scoop out all the pips and pith and add to the reserved orange liquid in the pan.

Bring to the boil for 6 minutes, then strain this liquid through a sieve into a bowl and press the pulp through with a wooden spoon. Pour half this liquid into a preserving pan. Cut the peel, with a sharp knife, into fine shreds. Add half the peel to the liquid in the preserving pan with the warm sugar. Stir over a low heat until all the sugar has dissolved, for about 10 minutes, then bring to the boil and bubble rapidly for 15- 25 minutes until setting point is reached.

Take pan off the heat and skim any scum from the surface. Leave the marmalade to stand in the pan for 20 minutes to cool a little and allow the peel to settle; then pot in sterilised jars.

Special Sandwich
by Chevy

Grandad sleeps a lot, but when he's awake, he's hilarious.

I get some memories of my grandad when I eat this lovely tiger bread sandwich. It makes my mouth water like a waterfall. I get memories since I was a little boy, age six.

Crushed up wheat tastes like heaven on a plate. It's nicer than the sweetest food in the whole of the land.

This sandwich is the most glorious thing I have ever had.

I like my warm, cosy house because my mum, dad and PS4 are there.

Sunday Sandwich
by Daisy

On Sunday I always have a cheese sandwich because it's my lazy day and it's quick to make.

I make it by myself. It started when I was seven but before I was seven, I had help with my mum.

I am always hungry, so I usually make cheese sandwiches because they are so yummy.

I make them in the kitchen because it's easy to clean up and it's where all the food is kept.

I only like cheddar but not too strong or too mild, with crusty bread and a scrape of butter. The cheddar is sometimes lumpy, so I keep grating until it's perfect and ready to eat.

The first time I made one, I was excited, but it was hard to use the cheese grater. I have never grated my skin because I am careful.

Cheese reminds me of rats and mice because they eat cheese and it's a popular food they eat. I would like a pet rat. If I had one, I would make it a cheese sandwich too!

TV Sandwich

INGREDIENTS

Tiger bread, preferably still warm
Whatever delicious items you want to put inside

METHOD

Slice the bread as thickly as you like and butter lightly

Slice your filling ingredients as thickly as you like.

Put the fillings in between the slices of bread. Press down.

Eat in front of the TV, wrapped in a blanket.

CHEESE

Doughnuts
by Steph

My sisters make the doughnuts in the kitchen. I have two sisters; one is 12 and the other is 13. I am 7.

The doughnut is soft when I pick it up and eat it with my hands. It is soft like my nan's dog, who is like a pillow. My favourite flavour is chocolate with chocolate sprinkles.

I am not sure when my sisters make them because I am on a dog walk, but the only reason why I have some is because they let me, and the reason for that is that they are kind.

My dad's favourite doughnuts are white chocolate with sprinkles. It makes me happy when I see them, pick them up, and eat them. It makes me feel like the sun when I look at it.

I love doughnuts. I eat them with my dad. I eat them at my house.

Doughnuts

INGREDIENTS

500g strong white bread flour
60g golden caster sugar
15g fresh yeast, crumbled
4 eggs
Zest of ½ lemon
2 tsp fine sea salt
125g unsalted butter, softened
Approx 2 litres sunflower oil, for frying
Caster sugar, for dusting

METHOD

Put 150ml water and all the dough ingredients (except the butter) into a mixer bowl with a beater paddle attachment.

Mix on medium speed for 8 mins or until the dough comes away from the sides and forms a ball.

Let the dough rest for 1 min.

Put the mixer back on medium and slowly add the butter about 25g at a time.

When all the butter is incorporated turn the mixer onto high for 5 mins.

The dough should be glossy, smooth, and very elastic.

Cover the bowl with cling film or a clean tea towel and leave to prove until it's doubled in size.

Knock back the dough briefly, recover, and refrigerate overnight.

Take the dough out and cut into 50g pieces (approx 20).

Roll the pieces into smooth tight buns and place on lightly floured baking tray.

Leave plenty of room between them.

Cover loosely with cling film and leave for 4 hrs or until doubled in size.

Fill a deep fat fryer or saucepan halfway with oil, heat to 180°C

Carefully place the donuts in the oil 2-3 at a time and fry for 2 mins until golden.

They may puff up and float so gently push them down after 1 min for even colour.

Remove from the oil and place on kitchen paper.

Toss the donuts in caster sugar while still warm.

If you want to fill your donuts make a small whole in the crease and pipe in a small amount.

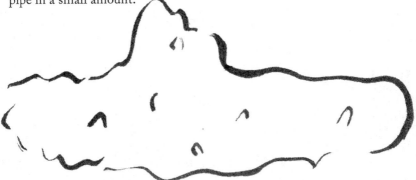

Lemon Fudge Brownie
by Zac

I love it so much; I wish for it 24/7.

Granny always needs to go shopping for sugar, butter, eggs, lemon juice, salt, and flour. Granny makes me feel warm and safe. She makes me feel good because the brownies she makes feel all warm in my tummy. Eating Lemon Fudge Brownie makes me feel loved.

The lemons feel nice on my fingers when I squeeze them except when I have a cut – then it stings! We put all the ingredients in a bowl and Granny lets me crack the eggs, and I get eggshells in the bowl. Then we mix it and I use the whisk; one time it splashed everywhere!

I'm allowed to cut the brownie when its warm and I sneak a taste. It smells so lemony! It's comforting. Granny is on a diet so she can't eat them, so I get more… I am happy!

Granny's home is like my home and that's where we make them.

Lemon Fudge Brownie

INGREDIENTS

2/3 of a cup of butter, softened
1 cup sugar
2 eggs
4 tbsp fresh lemon juice
Zest of two lemons
½ tsp salt
1¼ cups flour
1 cup icing sugar and juice and zest of one lemon, to glaze

METHOD

In a large mixing bowl, stir together the butter and sugar until combined.

Gradually add the eggs until just combined – don't overmix or the brownies will be tough.

Stir in the lemon juice, zest, salt, and flour, until a soft batter forms.

Spread the batter into a greased and lined pan.

Bake the brownies for 22-25 mins. Cool completely.

Make the glaze by whisking the icing sugar and lemon juice to form a spreadable paste.

Spread over the brownies and top with lemon zest.

When the glaze has set, cut into squares, and serve.

Jammy Dodgers
by Lynton

I went to Wagamama's with my daddy, my mummy, and my brother.

When we went to Wagamama's I had mini-ramen and we had a delicious, delightful meal.

It's been a long time since I ate a Jammy Dodger, and I would really like to have one soon. I like Chocolate Dodgers best.

Jammy Dodgers

INGREDIENTS

370ml jar strawberry jam
100g unsalted butter, softened
175g caster sugar, plus extra for sprinkling
1 large egg
1 tsp vanilla paste
200g plain flour

METHOD

To make the biscuits, mix together the butter and sugar in a bowl with a wooden spoon until well combined. Add the egg and vanilla, and continue to beat by hand until fully incorporated.

Tip the flour into the mixture and fold together until fully combined, then shape into a ball. Roll the dough out onto a floured sheet of baking parchment to a depth of around 5mm. Transfer the sheet to a baking tray and put in the fridge for 10 mins to firm up.

Remove from the fridge and press out your biscuits using a 6cm cutter. You will need 16 base biscuits and 16 top biscuits, with small holes or flowers of around 3cm cut out of them.

Once the shapes are cut out, arrange on 2 baking sheets lined with baking parchment and leave to cool in the fridge for 10 mins.

Heat oven to 190C/170C fan/gas 5. Bake the biscuits for 7 mins, then take them out of the oven and sprinkle the tops with caster sugar. Return all the biscuits to the oven and cook for a further 5 mins. Take out and allow to cool fully on a wire rack.

When cool, spread jam on the bottom biscuit and top with another biscuit, sandwiching them together.

My Cupcakes
by Albert

My mum and I made cupcakes. They were part of a big chocolate cake; we used them to make a short chimney, medium doors, and small windows. It looked amazing.

I love chocolate cupcakes, especially making them with my nan. She comes to visit in her campervan, and I like it when she helps. It smells nice and chocolatey when it's cooking.

I love licking the bowl and I like doing the delicious icing. I love the first taste – they are so sweet and squishy.

Chocolate Cupcakes

INGREDIENTS

100g plain flour
20g cocoa powder
140g caster sugar
1½ tsp baking powder
40g unsalted butter
120ml whole milk
1 egg
¼ tsp vanilla extract
Buttercream
Chocolate vermicelli (optional)

METHOD

Heat oven to 180°C. Put flour, cocoa powder, sugar, baking powder, pinch of salt and butter into a mixer and beat until sandy consistency

Whisk milk, egg, and vanilla extract together in a jug and slowly pour about half into flour mixture.

Beat to combine and turn mixture at a high speed.

Pour in the remaining liquid and mix for a couple more mins until smooth.

Spoon mixture into paper cases until 2/3 full.

Bake in preheated oven for 20-25 mins or until the sponge bounces back when touched

Shortbread!
by Spike

Shortbread is amazingly good. When I take a bite, it just melts in my mouth.

It's delicious with white chocolate because me and my mum tried it once and it was delicious. Now we use white chocolate more often.

Whenever I make it, I always do it with my mum, and I eat it with my family who are my mum, dad, aunty, granny, grumps, Ern, and Baby.

When I make it, I always smile.

Shortbread

INGREDIENTS

300g unsalted butter
135g light brown sugar
420g plain flour
½ tsp salt
2 tbsp caster sugar to sprinkle over
2 x bars white chocolate

METHOD

Line a 20cm square baking tin with baking paper, extend up and over edges.

Beat butter and sugar together until light & fluffy.

Sift flour and salt into separate bowl and add it to the butter and sugar a little at a time. Don't over beat!

Put the batter into the baking tin and prick all over the top with a fork.

Chill the batter in the fridge for 15 mins.

Pre heat oven to 170C.

Bake for 40-45 mins in the low oven so shortbread does not get too brown.

Remove from the oven and sprinkle with caster sugar.

While shortbread is still warm cut it into fingers.

Remove from tin when completely cool.

Melt the white chocolate in a bowl over a pan of simmering water

Dip one end of the shortbread finger into the chocolate to coat it.

Leave on a wire rack to cool.

The Terrible Chocolate Cupcake Disaster
by Jasmine

When I make chocolate cupcakes, it gives me memories of my nan in the kitchen. This makes me feel happy when I'm baking cupcakes, but it makes me feel sad at the same time because I miss her.

It used to be my nan helping me bake them, because they were her favourite, and she could only eat soft food because she had a couple of teeth missing. Once she ate a bag of crisps and one of her teeth fell out!

When I eat chocolate cupcakes it makes me think of my nan because she used to help me make them. I found the recipe off the internet, and she helped me bake it, when she could [still] walk. When she couldn't anymore, I still baked them for her.

When they come out of the oven, they smell so delicious they make me hungry.

The taste of cupcakes is so good, they make my mouth water (but not like dribbly water), and when I eat them, the taste is so delicious, especially when they turn out good and the texture is like melted chocolate.

The last time we made them, they didn't turn out too well. We left them in the oven too long and on top it came out hard, but on the bottom, it was soft and squishy. I still ate them, but I took the top off.

Chocolate Cupcakes

INGREDIENTS

175g plain flour
40g cocoa powder
1½ tsp baking powder
½ tsp bicarbonate of soda
250g caster sugar
Pinch of salt
100ml sunflower oil
2 large eggs
2 tsp of milk
125ml boiling water

FOR THE BUTTERCREAM

200g unsalted butter
130g icing sugar
15g cocoa powder
Handful of your favourite decorations

METHOD

Preheat the oven to 180°C and line 2 x 12 muffin tins with 18 paper cases.

Sift the flour, cocoa powder, baking powder and bicarbonate of soda into a large mixing bowl. Fold the caster sugar and a pinch of salt.

Add the sunflower oil, eggs and milk and beat until smooth.

Divide the mixture evenly between the cupcake cases.

Bake for 25 mins.

Take the cakes out and let them cool.

Decorate with buttercream and decorations.

Flapjack *by Leah*

Dear Flapjack,
Alive, I would play with you.
I would do anything with you and
I want to eat you,
And you make me happy every day.
I love you.
You fill me up.

Oh, Gooey Gooey Cookies *by Lois*

Oh, cookies,
your gooeyness melts in my mouth;
the chocolate fills me with joy.
I love watching you bake in the oven.
Oh, you're in ice cream – what better could there be?
You come in all different sizes…
Oh, cookies, you're the best.

Milkshake *by Oscar*

Oh, milkshake,
your taste makes my mouth water.
Oh, milkshake,
I would marry you if I could.

Olives *by Rosie*

O' olives, you are so sweet and oily
I love the way you're made so much.
I could eat a lot of you.
You are so exquisite when I put you in my mouth.
I would die if I didn't buy you from Lidl.
O' olives, you're so green and delicious.

Blue Cheese *by Chevy*

Oh, blue cheese, your smell attracts me from the next room.
Oh, blue cheese, I can eat a whole block in one gulp.
Oh, blue cheese, if you had legs, I'd marry you and then eat you.
Oh, blue cheese, you make me feel like I'm a vulture and you're
my prey.
Oh, blue cheese, when I see you my mouth drips.

Ode to Cheesy Chips *by Felicity R.*

Oh, cheesy chips, your cheese is stretchy and delicious,
and the chips are superbly crunchy.
I am drawn to you like a moth drawn to a light.
You are almost as amazing as a tiny, fluffy kitten.
You smell so terrific when you are frying
and when your cheese is melting,
I can't help but dip in a spoon and lick you clean.

Weetabix *by Diggory*

Weetabix and cereals
fills my tum every morning and
makes me feel energetic.

Yummy! Scrumptious

mmm...

Nom Nom!

DELICIOUS!

yum yum!. SWEET!

Oᵒᵒᵒₒₒₒₒ°°....

WOW!

TASTY

Nom Nom!

THE
BANK
OF
DREAMS

NIGHT
MARES

yummy!

The Project ～∿∿∿

The inspiration for this project came from a piece of writing by a teenage student at the International School in Florence, during a creative writing workshop there. Her 'food story' was a memory of breaking bread with her large Portuguese family. It was simple, moving, and uplifting, and thus sowed the seed for 'Food Glorious Food'.

Everyone has a food story, be it baking with parents or grandparents, a birthday meal, or a new taste sensation on holiday. Such stories have strong links and associations with family and friends, as the warmth and happiness provided by both food and the people we love, are interwoven to form the foundation of our lives. They are powerful stories - and memories - which begin at a young age. This is what we wanted to capture from our young writers at Salway Ash School.

Over a period of three weeks of intensive workshops we asked the pupils to taste the basis of all foods and use their language skills to describe those tastes. We asked them to choose a favourite food and write an Ode to it, using a light touch and figurative language.

We asked them to mine their own memories and traditions of food and share a recipe that meant something to them. We used mind mapping to unpick the feelings and senses associated with those recipes, as well as the settings and people involved. This creative process enabled the children to produce the most wonderful food stories from their lives, which in turn will enrich the lives of their readers.

We are enormously grateful to Leif Overment, headteacher at Salway Ash, who continues to champion reading and creative writing as a vital part of young people's education. In addition, we thank all the staff involved for their ongoing support.

The unique small-group mentoring offered by our team of volunteers makes what we do possible, and we thank Amberley Carter, Lu Orza, Raja Jarrah, Emily England, Lizzy Rhodes, Henry Bishop, Charlie Ryrie, Lorraine Colledge, Kate Asquith, Victoria Lazarevic and Claire Shaw for their commitment and nurturing of the children's words. And special thanks to food writer Lucy Brazier for her expertise and generosity of spirit in sharing her own food story.

'Food Glorious Food' provides nourishment for the soul and for the table, and we are privileged to be party to these young writers' precious stories and recipes. Badgers and Dragonflies: be proud!

Janis Lane
November 2022

About The Bank of Dreams & Nightmares

Our mission statement

Everyone's full of stories. Don't believe me? Well then off to bed and see for yourself. For when you sleep the stories in your head wake up. Your dreams and nightmares come alive and start to play in a world of infinite possibility and never-ending imagination. And then you wake up. And reality brings them crashing to an end, cruelly concluding all that could have been. Well we're here to put an end to that, or at least a beginning. 1000s and 1000s of beginnings. Hear ye hear ye! We at the Bank of Dreams & Nightmares want your stories. Bring them in, in all their absurd, weird and wonderful starts, middles or ends. And we'll keep your story alive, keep it going, bringing it out of your head and into the cold but illuminating light of day. And we won't stop there. Oh no. Every story deposited in the Bank of Dreams & Nightmares gets interest. Like any good bank we'll help your investment grow and grow. We'll give it eyes and ears to see and hear it, words to appreciate it, and applause to motivate it on. So believe in what's in your head, believe in what you can create, believe in your dreams and nightmares.

Our aim

get more kids writing and show them just
how far their words can take them.

By

making them realise their weird, wonderful,
absurd, ridiculous ideas are all story-worthy

Promising

that if they deposit them in our bank we'll bring
them to life and help them accrue interest
(i.e. eyes and ears to see and hear them)

The Inspiration

Valencia 826 in San Francisco

What we do

We are a registered charity in West Dorset and we offer FREE
creative writing workshops to children aged 7-18 in the West Dorset
area of the UK. We want to show children just how far their words
and stories can take them, so we work with industry professionals
to create inspirational workshops that all have a real world outcome.
How about writing a campaign for a cause you feel strongly about
and then seeing it made by professionals so you can present it to
local government or businesses? What if you wrote some song lyrics,
and then are able to see a real musical artist take your words and
make it into a real recording you can share with the world? Or how
about you become the lead defence lawyer for a special mock trial
in a real court house where your persuasive arguments determine

whether someone is guilty or not guilty? The possibilities are endless and at The Bank of Dreams & Nightmares; we want to have fun showing children that it all starts with an idea, a story, some words and where that can take you is the exciting part.

Our focus is on those children who are most under resourced, who normally do not have access to these types of things but deserve them just as much as anyone else.

We will be housed in a real bank in Bridport, but instead of money, we deal in the currency of stories, and at the back of the store, if you know where to look, is a secret door that leads to the writing centre where the real magic happens.

We work with both primary and secondary schools during term time providing one-off story writing workshops with the end result being published authors or broadcast podcasts! We also work in collaboration with secondary schools to develop longer term long projects where the outcome is a published anthology of the young writers' stories.

We offer after school clubs for children to develop their writing and get involved in longer workshop projects that currently range from creating their own quarterly newspaper to a sketch comedy workshop, with the final sketches being made by professional actors.

The Bank of Dreams & Nightmares is committed to practically addressing educational inequalities and the opportunity gap faced by young people from less advantaged backgrounds. We work in communities with high levels of socio-economic inequality, where we are providing a critical link between local schools, arts organisations, higher education institutions, and the commercial sector.

Our aim is to help children and young people to discover and harness the power of their own imaginations and creative writing skills. The Bank of Dreams & Nightmares strives to improve children's behaviour, engagement, essential life skills and wellbeing - the root causes of exclusion.

At its core The Bank of Dreams & Nightmares is also about something much broader and more inclusive: it is about using the creative practice of writing and storytelling to strengthen local children and teenagers from all backgrounds, to be resilient, creative, and successful shapers of their own lives.

Impact

Through our programmes, young writers will have felt listened to and have had their opinions valued and acted upon. We can demonstrate the impact creative writing has on young people. We provoke and empower them to think creatively and help them to unlock their imaginations. Then we publish their writing, providing purpose and value. The impact will demonstrate significant shifts in motivation, attitude, and behaviours - which in turn affects health, ambition, and resilience.

Our Workshops

Primary School
Storymaking workshop

In this two and a half hour workshop we work with a class collectively to create a story, whilst one of our volunteer illustrators brings the story to life as it happens. The first half of the session has the class of young writers voting and creating as a group, as one of our volunteers scribes the story for them. Once they get to the cliffhanger moment each writer then creates their own ending to the story, with the help of our story mentors. After the session we take the words and pictures and make them into a beautiful bound book with each participant getting their own author biog at the back and space to finish their individual ending. It is always a fun and lively session and the results have been wonderful.

Secondary School
Podcasting workshop

In this one-off workshop we work with a class of young writers to develop a personal essay about identity. The workshop normally lasts around four hours as we explore different aspects of the self and what it means to our writers. It is always a lively and interactive session and the final outcome is to record each essay as a podcast, which is broadcast via our soundcloud page.

Secondary School
10 Week Story Anthology

In this longer programme we work with one group of students to develop an anthology based on a chosen theme. We work closely with the school to decide on a theme which complements the curriculum for the chosen year group. At the end of the six weeks we make the final anthology into a published book, one of which you are reading now. All the proceeds from the sales of the book go directly back into the charity.

The Vault Newspaper

This is our after school workshop that takes place every Thursday during term time after school. Here we work with a group of young writers between 10 and 15 years of age to create a quarterly subscription-based newspaper. In the issue we look back at the news from the last three months and the writers share their perspectives on the news stories that they have selected.

We have many more workshops being developed, and will hopefully be able to share them with you all very soon.

People

Founder
Nick Goldsmith

Creative learning manager
Ed Swift

Volunteer Coordinator
Alex Green

Board of Directors
Mick Smith
Simon Deverell
Joel Collins
Niki McCretton
Simon Hawkins

Our Volunteers

There is absolutely no way any of this would be possible without our incredible volunteers. These incredible people work in all realms from story mentoring to illustrating and beyond. They range in age, background and expertise but all have a shared passion for our work with young people. We salute you!

It's always a good time to give!

We need your help

We are always seeking new volunteers to help out either as story mentors, illustrators, or simply as experts in their fields. It is very simple to join as a volunteer, and we try and make it a lot of fun in the process. You do not need to be a writer or have an educational background, you just need to be able to listen and encourage our young writers to express themselves.

Please fill out our online application to let us know how you may be able to help, and to come along to one of our training sessions. Tea and cake provided!

**More information at
thebankofdreamsandnightmares.org/volunteering**

Other ways to give

Whether it's loose change or heaps of cash, a donation of any size will help The Bank of Dreams & Nightmares continue to offer a variety of FREE writing workshops to children in the West Dorset area.
Please make a donation at:
thebankofdreamsandnightmares.org/donate
Or email us at **nick@thebankofdreamsandnightmares.org**
to discuss how you may be able to help.